JOHN WITTICH AND RON PHILLIPS

Discovering Off-Beat Walks in London

D0237354

SHIRE PUBLICATIONS LTD

British Library Cataloguing in Publication Data:
Wittich, John
  Discovering Off-beat Walks in London. –
  6 Rev.ed. – (Discovering Series; No. 63)
  I. Title II. Phillips, Ron III. Series
  914. 2104859
  ISBN 0-7478-0263-7

The cover design is by Felix Partridge. The photographs are by Cadbury Lamb.

Published in 1995 by Shire Publications Ltd, Cromwell House, Church Street, Princes Risborough, Buckinghamshire HP27 9AA, UK.
Copyright © 1969 by John Wittich and Ron Phillips and 1995 by John Wittich. First published 1969; reprinted 1970. Second edition 1973. Third edition 1977; reprinted 1979. Fourth edition 1980; reprinted 1984. Fifth edition 1990. Sixth edition 1995. Number 63 in the Discovering series. ISBN 0 7478 0263 7.

Printed in Great Britain by CIT Printing Services, Press Buildings, Merlins Bridge, Haverfordwest, Dyfed SA61 1XF.

Contents

Walk 1   **Around London Wall**   **5**
St Paul's Underground Station—St Martin Le Grand
—Aldersgate—Gresham Street—Noble Street—London
Wall—Wood Street—Cheapside.

Walk 2   **Lincoln's Inn Fields**   **14**
Royal Courts of Justice, The Strand—Aldwych—
Houghton Street—Portugal Street—Portsmouth Street—
Lincoln's Inn—Serle Street—Carey Street—Bell
Yard—Temple Bar.

Walk 3   **Thomas More's Chelsea**   **24**
Chelsea Town Hall, King's Road—Glebe Place—
Upper Cheyne Row—Cheyne Row—Lordship Place—
Lawrence Street—Justice Walk—Old Church Street —
Margaret Roper Gardens—Danvers Street—Battersea
Bridge—Beaufort Street—King's Road—Paultons
Square.

Walk 4   **Fleet Street and its tributaries**   **32**
Temple Bar—Prince Henry's Room—St Dunstan's-
in-the-West—Johnson Court—Gough Square—Fleet
Street—Cheshire Cheese—Salisbury Square—St
Bride's Church—Ludgate Circus.

Walk 5   **The Precincts of Westminster Abbey**   **40**
St James's Park Underground Station—Queen Anne's
Gate—Dartmouth Street—Tothill Street—Broad
Sanctuary—St Margaret's Church—Old Palace Yard—
Millbank—Dean Stanley Street—Smith Square—Lord
North Street—Cowley Street—Barton Street—Great
College Street—Dean's Yard—Westminster Abbey.

Walk 6   **In the steps of the Black Friars**   **50**
Blackfriars Underground Station—Mermaid Theatre—
St Benet's Church—Queen Victoria Street—Godliman
Street—Knightrider Street—Carter Lane Dean's
Court—Wardrobe Place—St Andrew's Hill—Ireland
Yard—Playhouse Yard—Church Entry—Carter Lane—
Blackfriars Lane—The Black Friar public house.

Walk 7   Mayfair—on the course of the Tyburn   58
Green Park Underground Station—Piccadilly—
Whitehorse Street—Shepherd Market—Curzon
Street—Queen Street, Mayfair—Charles Street—
Berkeley Square—Hill Street—Farm Street—South
Audley Street—Grosvenor Square.

Walk 8   The Great Fire of London   68
The Monument—Monument Street—St Mary at
Hill—Eastcheap—Philpot Lane—Lime Street—
Leadenhall Market—Leadenhall Street—Cornhill—St
Peter's Church—St Michael's Church—St Michael's
Alley—Castle Court—Ball Court—Birchin Lane—
Change Alley—Lombard Street—King William
Street—The Monument.

Index of places   79

The memorial to Temple Bar in Fleet Street.

4

Walk 1
Around London Wall

St Paul's Underground Station—St Martin Le Grand—Aldersgate—Gresham Street—Noble Street—London Wall—Wood Street—Cheapside.

To walk the entire length of the old city wall one would have to tramp over three miles, starting at the Tower of London and, by following a roughly half-circular course, ending up at Blackfriars before covering the length of Upper and Lower Thames Streets. However, for the purpose of this walk we have chosen an area in which several portions of the wall can still be clearly seen.

It was late in the second century AD that a wall was first constructed of stone around the then perimeter of the City of London. When completed it enclosed some 330 acres (133 hectares) of land, making it the fifth largest city in the Roman Empire.

As London had no stone quarries of its own the stone was 'imported' from Kent, being called Kentish ragstone. The outside faces of the wall were made up of stones which had been squared off and so presented a fairly smooth surface. In between the facings was poured concrete and other stones to make up the hard centre. In front was a ditch; behind, on the city side, an earthen ramp was built as an added protection against any enemy trying to burrow through. The wall's height was from 30 to 35 feet (9 to 10.5 metres), and along the inner side there was a sentry walk along which soldiers guarding the city would keep watch.

Our walk starts from **St Paul's Underground Station**, where St Martin Le Grand meets Newgate Street and Cheapside.

The name St Martin Le Grand reminds one that here, in the middle ages, was one of London's many monasteries. The bell in the church tower here would ring out every evening to tell the citizens of London to 'cover their fires, shut up their shutters and go to bed'. This was the curfew, rung from several of the church towers throughout medieval times. Like so many other monasteries, St Martin Le Grand was dissolved in the sixteenth century and its stone used for other purposes; much of it went to help build the first Somerset House in the Strand. The site is now occupied by the offices of British Telecom. On the side of the building there is a plaque that reads 'From this site Guglielmo Marconi made the first public transmission of wireless signals on 27 July 1896'.

Walking up St Martin Le Grand, past the British Telecom offices, one comes to the church of **St Botolph's, Aldersgate (1)**, one of the three remaining London churches dedicated to this Saxon saint from Boston, Lincolnshire. As with the others, this church is just outside the place where the city gate once stood, which is not at all surprising as Botolph is a patron saint of the huntsmen who would have travelled through the gates of the city to hunt in the forests of Middlesex and Essex. The present church dates from the eighteenth century and is one of the few churches not to have been rebuilt by Sir Christopher Wren after the Great Fire of London of 1666. The earliest record of the church dates from 1260 when the patrons of the living were the canons of the nearby St Martin's Priory. The churchwardens and parochial records are among the earliest of the City; dating from 1466, they are kept in the Guildhall Library, where they may be seen on application. John Stow in his *Survey of the Cities of London and Westminster* records that in 1377 the Brotherhood of St Fabian and St Sebastian was founded in the parish. There are several monuments from the previous church on the walls inside the church. The present building was built in 1754 by an unknown architect but possibly by George Dance, who designed St Botolph, Aldgate, at that time.

One of the stained glass windows in St Botolph's, Aldersgate, showing Princess Anne, later Queen Anne, being received by the Bishop of London.

Walk 1. Around London Wall

1. St Botolph's, Aldersgate
2. Aldersgate plaque
3. St Anne and St Agnes
4. Roman city wall
5. Roman barracks
6. Barber Surgeons' Hall
7. St Giles', Cripplegate
8. Bomb plaque
9. Roman city wall
10. Elsing Priory
11. Police station
12. St Alban's tower
13. Wood Street Comptor
14. St Peter's railings

Some of the memorial plaques in Postmen's Park.

There is a similarity between the two buildings. All the stained glass of the south aisle is modern and its theme is the history of the church.

In the churchyard, known familiarly as the Postmen's Park, can be found the **George Frederick Watts Memorial Cloisters**. In these cloisters are commemorated many deeds of heroism by everyday people who lost their lives trying to save others. One plaque, for instance, tells the story of a young girl in Union Street in the borough who, having saved three children from a fire, died while trying to rescue a fourth child.

Retracing one's steps a few yards, on a building almost opposite the church is a blue plaque (**2**) placed by the City Corporation to mark the spot where Aldersgate once stood.

The origin of the name **Aldersgate** is either because it was one of the older gates of the city (it was the north gate of the Roman city when there were only four gates in the city wall), or because the building, or rebuilding, of the gate was sponsored by someone whose name was Ealdred. There is mention of it by name in a document of 1289, which would make it concerned with an order of the same century which read 'All gates of the City are to be open by day, and at each gate there are to be two sergeants to open the same, skilful men, and fluent of speech, who are to keep watch on persons coming and going so that no evil shall befall the City'. A similar order of the fourteenth century commanded that 'all gates are to be closed every night on the hour of the Curfew being rung'. Also, regulations were made that gates should be guarded by twelve men by day and twenty-four by night who were to be 'able-bodied, well instructed and well armed'. Originally, in the middle ages, every able-bodied man in the city was made to 'stand guard at the gates', but later the wealthier merchants paid others to do their tour of duty. When the gate was rebuilt in the early part of the seventeenth century it was quite a handsome building, three storeys high, with flanking towers. On the outer face was a statue of James I of England in his Chair of State, recalling that as James VI of Scotland he passed through this gateway on his acceptance of the throne of England. The gate was finally demolished in the eighteenth century, but not before a printer by the name of John Day had used it as his printing works. Tradition relates that John Day would awaken his apprentices each morning by entering their sleeping quarters and announcing 'Awake for it is Day'!

Moving down on the left-hand side of the road, back towards St Paul's Station, one comes to **Gresham Street**, which reminds us of one of the great names in the history of the city – Sir Thomas Gresham, founder of the Royal Exchange and Gresham College.

Just inside Gresham Street is the church of **St Anne and St Agnes (3)**. Severely damaged in the Second World War, it was carefully rebuilt to the original designs of Sir Christopher Wren and is now used by a Latvian congregation. Note the large 'A' on the church tower's weathervane. Once this church was described as 'St Anne's-in-the-willows', a pleasant reminder of a nearby stream that has long since disappeared. John Wesley preached here twice in the eighteenth century: on the last occasion he wrote in his diary 'I fear they bear me no longer' – he had been told not to preach there again.

A few yards from the church is **Noble Street**, named after Thomas Le Noble who lived here in the fourteenth century. Walk up the street and you will find extensive remains of the **Roman city wall (4)**. Notice particularly the portion nearest to the church where you can see the city wall joined with that of a fort which was built before the wall itself. Notice too the little culvert built into the lower portion allowing a small stream to pass through without undermining the strength of the wall. Follow the line of the wall and you will find several stretches of it running parallel to Noble Street. You will then come to the broad modern roadway called London Wall. This is a post-war thoroughfare built to allow modern transport to move more freely where once the Roman chariots were housed.

Crossing **London Wall** one sees the Museum of London to the left. But before taking to the upper pedestrian ways seek out the entrance to the old fort of London, now nestling by the side of an underground car park. Choose your time well and you will be able to descend to the level of the Roman city and see the foundations of

The bastion of the city wall, viewed from the upper walkway.

the old guardhouse of London's first fortified barracks (**5**). Enquiries should be made at the reception desk of the nearby Museum of London regarding access to the guardhouse remains. Leaving the fort find the nearest stairway which will take you to the upper pedestrian walks and you will find yourself in twenty-first century London. Look down into the square behind at the **Barber Surgeons' Hall (6**), built right into the city wall itself. It is hard to think today of this city company being responsible not only for haircuts and shaving but also for blood-letting, the 'cure' for so many ills of previous ages. This is why barbers had poles outside their establishments painted red, white and blue; white for the shaving and haircuts, red for the blood and blue for the veins; signs which have now almost disappeared from the streets of London. Over the top of the flats is the tower of **St Giles' Cripplegate (7**), one of the largest parish churches in the city. Find another staircase nearby, descend to ground level via these steps, pass the Barber Surgeons' Hall and pay a visit to the church. We pass on the way another blue plaque which shows us where Cripplegate once stood, but we shall return there later.

St Giles is another patron saint of huntsmen and again, appropriately, is found just outside the city wall on the road to the forests. The church was rebuilt after a fire in the middle of the sixteenth century, escaped damage in the Great Fire of 1666, only to be completely gutted in the bombing of 1940. Here Oliver Cromwell was married to Elizabeth Bourchier; here Milton was buried, in the church which earlier saw him re-united to his first wife, Mary Powell. Near the churchyard is one of the bastions of the city wall and an attractive strip of water.

Retracing our steps, we come to **Fore Street**, and on the side of Roman House is a plaque **(8)** which tells us that here fell the city's first explosive bomb in the Second World War. Notice the modern, Roman-style mosaic on the raised entrance platform. Underneath the building, not accessible to the public, in the parking area cars are left against the city wall built by the Romans. Was the wall here ever used to park chariots against it? Returning to the upper pedestrian way, we find the **Cripplegate plaque**, already mentioned. Like Aldersgate this too has alternative origins for its name, but it most probably derives from the Anglo-Saxon word *crepel* which means den or underground passage. There was an underground entrance to the city here in the middle ages. Once the gates of the city were closed after the curfew had ceased to ring there was only one place you could legally enter and that was here at Cripplegate. You had to prove your identity in some way and, provided the guards were satisfied that you belonged to the city, and had, as you maintained, only been seeing your girl friend home, being late back because of a tiff, you were then let back in. Like others this gate too was maintained as a prison at one time; also it is on record as having been used as a dwelling house for the Common Cryer of the City of London. At one time the gate was rebuilt at the expense of the Worshipful Company of Brewers, which doubtless suited their purposes very well, as it led to the fields outside the city wall where the apprentices and others practised the noble art – and thirsty work – of warfare. Like Aldersgate, Cripplegate was demolished in the eighteenth century and sold for ninety pounds.

Now turn left by the side of Roman House, and you will come to one of the most magnificent stretches of London's **city wall (9)** still clearly visible. Carefully ascend the stairway to the side of the wall and you will be able to imagine quite easily how formidable a cliff the wall would have presented anybody wishing to enter illegally.

Retrace your steps to the roadway and another set of stairs which lead to the upper walks once more. Look back now, downwards to the wall, tiny against the great modern buildings towering over it. One wonders which will last longer! Almost immediately behind you now stand the remains of yet another monastic establishment, the former **Elsing Priory (10)**, founded in the fourteenth century by Sir William de Elsing as a hospital for one hundred blind men who were turned out at the time of the dissolution of the monasteries. It then became a private dwelling until a fire in the latter half

11

of the sixteenth century destroyed most of it, except the chapel which was used by the nearby parish of St Alphage as its church. It was finally demolished in 1924, leaving this rare example of medieval architecture to be later surrounded by modern office blocks.

While remaining in the upper walks cross the bridge over London Wall by Bastion House and descend on the other side into **Wood Street**, probably once the resort of woodworkers. Today, however, it contains the **City of London police station (11)**, which has as its front door neighbour the tower of **St Alban's (12)**, all that remains of a church rebuilt in the seventeenth century by Inigo Jones, and later repaired by Sir Christopher Wren after the Great Fire of London. It has been converted into an office and flat with a roof garden.

Cross over Gresham Street and, continuing down Wood Street, one finds on the left-hand side an entrance marked Mitre Court, the end of which opens into a courtyard. In the centre stands the entrance to the old **Wood Street Comptor (13)** or prison, now used as a store for wine, etc.

Returning once more to Wood Street, turn left and you will soon

Left: *All that remains of Elsing Priory on London Wall.*

Right: *The tower of St Alban's in Wood Street.*

The Wood Street Comptor.

find yourself by some **iron railings (14)** marking the site of the church of St Peter's West Chepe. The church itself was not rebuilt after the Great Fire but the symbol of St Peter, the crossed keys, can still be seen entwined in the railings. A few yards further on you are in Cheapside, 100 yards (90 metres) from where you started this walk.

Walk 2
Lincoln's Inn Fields

Royal Courts of Justice, The Strand—Aldwych—Houghton Street —Portugal Street—Portsmouth Street—Lincoln's Inn— Serle Street—Carey Street—Bell Yard—Temple Bar.

Although this walk is directed to the highly interesting off-beat precinct adjacent to Lincoln's Inn, we shall also be wandering in and out of streets which were once part of central London's worst slum. Consisting of some 28 acres (11 hectares), containing, for example, Wych Street, Holywell Street and Clare Market, this area was notorious for its gin-houses, brothels and thieves' kitchens. So old and mouldering were the buildings in these shambles that often, during the 1900-5 clearances, houses deprived of their neighbours collapsed of their own accord. Many of the nineteenth-century alleys still remain as 'rights of way' and a walker with an imaginative eye might be able to catch for a moment the horrors of the 'good old days'.

As the walk commences at the **Law Courts (1)**, or the Royal Courts of Justice – to give them their official title, perhaps the best vantage point would be the island in the centre of the roadway. At a first viewing the building gives the impression of being a very old baronial castle – Scottish perhaps – complete with spires and turrets. However, one would be greatly mistaken, since the complex dates from 1874-80, before which time the Royal Courts of Justice were based at the Palace of Westminster.

Designed by George Edmund Street, a pupil of Sir George Gilbert Scott, the Courts architecturally represent 'the last fling of the Gothic Revival', a period which gave London the Houses of Parliament, St Pancras Station and a host of similar structures. The styling was extremely romantic, with pleasant arcading, a minimum of symmetrical layout and no mean distribution of statuary. The site is one of 8 acres (3 hectares) with a perimeter of about half a mile, and prior to the preparation for its present purpose was covered by thirty-three streets and bye-ways of the Wych Street rookery containing three or four hundred houses and four thousand people.

The interior includes thirty courthouses of various sizes, all serving the Supreme Court of Judicature for England and Wales. Cases heard here cover three divisions of law, namely: Chancery, Queen's Bench, and Probate, Divorce and Admiralty, these last

Walk 2. Lincoln's Inn Fields

1. Law Courts
2. St Clement Danes
3. London School of Economics
4. Old Curiosity Shop
5. Conyingham's house
6. The Ship tavern
7. Soane's Museum
8. Execution site
9. Royal College of Surgeons
10. Lincoln's Inn gateway
11. Statue of Thomas More
12. Boundary stones
13. Six-bay house of 1731
14. Temple Bar

three always being grouped together. Criminal cases, except for appeals, are heard elsewhere, principally at the Central Criminal Court, more popularly known as the Old Bailey.

Look up over the entrance gateway and one can see three statues. The central one is of Christ with His hand raised in blessing, the supreme lawmaker; on the left can be seen King Solomon, and on the right is King Alfred. (The outside rear of the building in Casey Street has a statue of Moses and the Ten Commandments.)

The general public are allowed to visit only the Great Hall without an escort. In no circumstances are cameras allowed inside the building. (Persons with photographic equipment are advised to leave one member of their party outside with all their cameras and then to change over so that another can see inside the hall as well.) Visitors are also advised that a security screening is in operation at the entrance to the Hall. Once inside the Hall visitors can admire the spaciousness of the area covered and the fine detail of the ornamental work. A statue of George Edmund Street, the architect, can be seen on the right-hand side of the hall. The carvings on the plinth, by Armsted, show various craftsmen working on the building. The Courts are the setting for a special ceremony in October every year. The City Solicitor presents to the Queen's Remembrancer six horseshoes and sixty-one nails as rent for 'The Forge' that once stood 'in the neighbourhood of the Strand'. It is possible that the original forge was used by the Knights Templar when they occupied the area now covered by the Temple. The same shoes and nails have been changing hands for 500 years!

Still on the central island in the roadway, before starting the walk, note the bollards at the curbside, designed to match the Gothic Law Courts and, above all, a most magnificent lamp post, picked out in gold and bearing a veritable candelabrum of lights.

On the same island one finds the very realistic figure of Dr Samuel Johnson facing Fleet Street and the quarter of the city in which he became a legend. He holds in his hand the first dictionary of the English language, which he had compiled. Nearby a plaque shows us the site of the Holywell which gave its name to a nearby street as well as to some not-so-holy water percolating up through the graveyard.

We can now examine the church of **St Clement Danes (2)**. It is dedicated to the saint who was martyred by being bound to an anchor and cast overboard. The latter part of the church's name springs from the time when, after the Danes had been driven out of England, those who had married Englishwomen and remained here were ordered to live in this district. It is thought by some that Harold I, a Dane by birth, was buried here. Most Londoners feel a close affinity to St Clements because of the familiar nursery rhyme

*St Clement
Danes
church is the
Central
Church of
the Royal Air
Force.*

'Oranges and Lemons', the tune of which has long been rung on
the bells. Although the pre-Great Fire St Clements escaped the fate
of so many London churches during that catastrophe, by 1680 it
was unsafe enough to merit rebuilding and Christopher Wren, then
at the peak of his creativity, produced a structure of rare beauty.
James Gibbs completed the church by adding the steeple in the
eighteenth century. During the night of 10th May 1941, the church
was reduced to a shell; the famous bells, except for the Sanctus,
were destroyed too.

In 1955 work was started on restoration, Wren's original design
being kept in mind, and now we have a superb 'Wren reproduc-
tion'. The church was re-dedicated and now serves as a memorial
to the Royal Air Force; £150,000 was raised from the Commonwealth and other allied nations to cherish the memory of those who
had defended our freedom. The Royal Family was present for the
re-dedication in October 1958 as were representatives of the air

forces of the Commonwealth. The floor of the church contains over 700 slate carvings of badges of the squadrons and units of the RAF and there are 800 hassocks, all of different embroidery designs, that were made and presented by men and women all over the world. Three windows in contemporary stained glass dominate the altar end of the church. But above all it is the glorious interior, in silver grey and white, and the golden dome of the apse that draw the eye.

The famous bells, what was left of them, were taken back to the Whitechapel Bell Foundry, where they had been manufactured in 1693. They were recast and today ring out the nursery rhyme at 9 a.m., 12 noon, 3 p.m. and 6 p.m., just as they have done for nearly three centuries. The carillon also includes 'The Old Hundredth' and 'The Royal Air Force March' in its repertoire. Every year on a Thursday in late March the children from the nearby St Clement Danes Church of England Primary School in Drury Lane attend a service at the end of which they all receive one orange and one lemon. The exact date can be verified by telephoning the school secretary on 0171-836 3787.

Crossing from the island towards Australia House we turn right, crossing over the road which is one of London's finest crescents – **Aldwych**. Created at the turn of the nineteenth century by the clearance of the Wych Street slums, Aldwych has many fine commercial buildings and is dominated at the central portion by the great complex of Bush House, named after Irving T. Bush, an American businessman, and designed by another American, Harvey W. Corbett. The main entrance facing the wide vista of Kingsway is topped by two very large statues representing the friendship of the English-speaking peoples. One of these suffered damage during the war but was not repaired because the 'war-wounds', so it was thought, drew the alliance closer. The building houses the BBC's External Radio Services, tenants here since 1940.

A few yards further on we enter Houghton Street and the 'revolutionary' precinct of the **London School of Economics (3)**. Founded in 1895 to promote 'the study and advancement of Economics or Political Economy, Political Science or Political Philosophy, Statistics, Sociology, History, Geography, and any subject cognate to any of these', it was the brain-child of Henry Hunt Hutchinson, a founder member of the Fabian Society. On his death in 1894 he left instructions for Sidney Webb to 'dispose of the residue of my estate for socially progressive purposes'. So the LSE was born! Part of London University, the LSE has produced many of the father figures of the Labour Party; it continues in this tradition, with its students always in the vanguard of protest on every issue of political importance.

The entrance to the London School of Economics and Political Science is surmounted by a shield depicting a beaver, subsequently adopted by the students as their mascot.

Continue left into Clare Market, once heart of the great slums, prior to the clearances. The name stems from John Holles, Earl of Clare, who in 1617 was granted the right to set up a market, around which the mean streets grew, as did the poor and miserable local population. Strype in 1720 described the area as being 'very considerable and well served with provisions, both (human?) and fish; for besides the butchers in the shambles, it is much resorted to by the country butchers and higglers'. Higgle is a less common word for haggle.

We go next to the **Old Curiosity Shop (4)**, having turned from Clare Market into Portugal Street and then into Portsmouth Street. At the end we see the tiny shop that has long been famous as one of London's main tourist attractions. There are those who would quarrel with the claim that Charles Dickens used this as his model. But he did know the little shop very well, not on its present site, but at its previous location behind the National Gallery. Whether the visitor is sceptical or not, the 'home of little Nell and her grandfather' is certainly worth a visit.

Now leaving the shop on our right, we cross **Sardinia Street** to the west side of Lincoln's Inn Fields. The street name is a memory of the Catholic chapel of the Sardinian Embassy, sited here, which twice served as a target for anti-popery rioters. Dickens refers to the final outbreak of 1760 in his book *Barnaby Rudge*.

Lincoln's Inn Fields were first built upon in 1618 on this west side, and battle commenced between those who sought to profit by building houses, and the Society of Lincoln's Inn, whose members owned the land. During this period Inigo Jones, the famous architect, was commissioned to lay out the central portion as a garden. Two hundred and fifty years later Lincoln's Inn Fields were purchased by the London County Council and thrown open to the public. It is now maintained by the London Borough of Camden with Lincoln's Inn Fields Association keeping a watching brief over any matters that may affect the well-being of the 'square'.

Before entering the gardens, we should continue along the west side. **Numbers 57 and 58** were originally a 1640 house remodelled by the great Leoni in 1730 and divided into two a few years later. The latter house was lived in by John Forster, Dickens's biographer, and the novelist often came here to give readings from his books. Dickens mentions the house in one of his stories, as the home of Mr Tulkinghorn, a character in *Bleak House*.

Numbers 59 and 60 (5), attributed to Inigo Jones and built for Sir David Conyingham in 1640, were also eventually split into a pair of houses. **Newcastle House** is on the corner at Number 66 and, as the plaque at the top indicates, is by Sir Edwin Lutyens, who copied this building from a previous one by Sir John Vanbrugh, builder of Blenheim Palace for the Duke of Marlborough. One of the well-known names associated with the house is the Society for the Promoting of Christian Knowledge, founded in 1696 'to assist in disseminating Christian Knowledge among the nations of the world wherever the Anglican Church is at work'. (The Society now operates from the former Holy Trinity Church in Marylebone Road.) At the side, in Remnant Street, the pleasant arcading over the pavement is all that is left of Vanbrugh's original work. Continue for a moment into Gate Street and at the end we find a tavern of great historic interest – **The Ship (6)**. Here, during the Catholic persecution, religious services were held, thanks to a sympathetic proprietor. Worshippers would enter the bars as ordinary customers, call for ale and pass into the parlour. If, however, suspected government spies were around, the congregation would get a discreet wink from the potman and hold their ales until the danger was over. The service would be temporarily abandoned, with the priest hidden somewhere upstairs.

Retracing our steps, we turn left along the north side of the Fields to Number 13. This is the **Sir John Soane's Museum (7)**, an incredible collection of antiquities left *in situ* by the famous Georgian architect. Here, amongst other delights, one can find the alabaster sarcophagus of Pharaoh Seti I, father of Rameses the Great, a death mask of Sarah Siddons, and an astounding picture

The Royal College of Surgeons in Lincoln's Inn Fields.

gallery notable for the two series of paintings by William Hogarth: 'The Rake's Progress' and 'The Election'.

Cross the road now and enter the central path into the gardens. At the centre, under the roof of a shelter, can be found a brass plaque marking an execution site (**8**). This is where, in 1683, Lord William Russell was beheaded for his complicity in the Rye House plot, and where, about a hundred years before, Anthony Babington and fourteen others were hanged, drawn and quartered for trying to procure the escape of Mary, Queen of Scots, after her imprisonment by Elizabeth I. Walk through to the other side of the gardens and, before turning left, look at the fine building by Sir Charles

The gateway to Lincoln's Inn.

Barry constructed in 1835 for the **Royal College of Surgeons (9)**, with a portico by George Dance.

Ahead now can be seen the gateway into **Lincoln's Inn (10)**, one of the four Inns of Court. These serve as chambers for those practising at the bar and here aspiring barristers 'keep terms' by dining in hall on a specific number of occasions during their period of training. The Inn derives its name from Henry de Lacey, Earl of Lincoln (died 1311), who turned his town house over to law students and legal practitioners. The oldest building in the vast complex is the 1491 **Old Hall**, which was extended in 1624 by Inigo Jones and restored in 1928. It contains a large religious painting by Hogarth. The enormous **New Hall** of 1843 is by Philip Hardwick, styled in neo-Tudor and bearing the date and the initials of the architect in brick diapering. The library next door is thought to have the oldest and most comprehensive collection of law books in the world. Although one is allowed to walk, by privilege and not by right, around the precincts, the chapel is the only building open to the public. It is well worth a visit since it is also the work of Inigo Jones and was finished in 1623; it is unusual in that the chapel is raised over a ground-level crypt. The plan of the burials in the undercroft makes interesting reading and can be found attached to the wall near the stairs leading up to the chapel. Strolling about the pleasant seventeenth- and eighteenth- century squares and buildings of Lincoln's Inn is a delightful way of passing time.

Leave again by the gate and turn left into Serle Street and left again into Carey Street, noting the statue of **Sir Thomas More** (**11**) over a doorway on the corner. It stands in a recess of the building that was the first Lyons' Corner House in London. Carey Street was first developed in the seventeenth century, when it led to the house of Sir George Carey. The name of this street is associated with empty pockets, for until recently the Bankruptcy Court was one of its buildings, but there is still much of interest here. Within yards of the corner we find the **Seven Stars** pub, a reminder of the days when the Dutch, engaged in welding the seven Netherlands provinces into a nation, sometimes took refuge in England. Next, a little further on, look out for the two oldest **parish boundary stones** (**12**) in central London. They are at the bottom of a wall at pavement level; one marks the parish of St Clement Danes by means of an anchor; the other bears the letters SDW — St Dunstan's in the West. The shop close by the stones, A. Woodhouse & Son, displays in its window a silver mouse trap. These splendid traps were placed near to the pillow of a lady's bed in order to catch any mouse that may have been attracted to her hair! When a lady's hair was 'dressed up' in earlier times it would be 'whitened' with flour. Frequent use of flour encouraged mice and the trap was placed at the bedside to catch them! Finally, before turning right into Bell Yard, there is a fine **six-bay house of 1731** (**13**), perfectly symmetrical – except for its drainpipe!

Bell Yard, entered now, is named after a long-since vanished tavern. Samuel Pepys, the diarist, refers to his first dabble at gambling in a house here. Charles Dickens in 1831 used Number 5 during his early days as a reporter and, as might be expected, later used the Yard for a scene in *Bleak House*. At the end of Bell Yard we have reached **Temple Bar** (**14**), which is described at the beginning of Walk 4 and is only a stone's throw from where we started.

Walk 3
Thomas More's Chelsea

Chelsea Town Hall, King's Road—Glebe Place—Upper Cheyne Row—Cheyne Row—Lordship Place—Lawrence Street—Justice Walk—Old Church Street—Margaret Roper Gardens — Danvers Street—Battersea Bridge—Beaufort Street —King's Road—Paultons Square.

Thomas More, or, to give him his full title, Saint Sir Thomas More, was born in Milk Street, off Cheapside, in 1478. His father was a judge and it was natural that young Thomas should follow in his father's footsteps, as he did when he became a law student at Lincoln's Inn. In 1501 he was called to the bar, and three years later entered Parliament, beginning a highly successful career which culminated in his acceptance of the Lord Chancellorship in 1529. Meanwhile, he had married Jane Colt, by whom he had three daughters and one son, but Jane died young and More then married the widow Alice Middleton. As a judge he was incorruptible, as Henry VIII soon found out when he tried to persuade More that his marriage to Catherine of Aragon was invalid; More resigned the Chancellorship and retired from public life to his house in Chelsea; he was later tried, found guilty of treason, and executed at Tower Hill on the 6th July 1535. His last words to the spectators around the scaffold were: 'I am the King's good servant, but God's first'.

During the past decades King's Road, Chelsea, once a private road used only by the king on his way to Hampton Court, has become noted for its fashion shops. Our walk starts at the former **Town Hall (1)** of the Borough of Chelsea, now merged with the Royal Borough of Kensington to form the Royal Borough of Kensington and Chelsea. The Town Hall was the work of the architect J. M. Brydon and dates from 1886, with extensions at the start of the twentieth century. We turn left and walk down the road to what was once one of the largest public houses in London, the **Six Bells (2)**. It is now Henry J. Bean's bar and grill.

Opposite is the **Old Chelsea burial ground** that was given to the 'People of Chelsea' in 1736 by Sir Hans Sloane. It contains many monuments, including one to Cipriani, the Italian painter, whose works include the panels of the Lord Mayor of London's coach and the Gold State Coach that has been used for every Coronation since the reign of George III.

Crossing Oakley Street one finds, still in King's Road, a group of early eighteenth-century houses which offer the visitor some

Walk 3. Thomas More's Chelsea

1. Old Town Hall
2. The former Six Bells
3. Argyll House
4. Hunting Lodge
5. Upper Cheyne Row
6. Church of Our Most Holy Redeemer
7. Carlyle's house
8. Monmouth House
9. Smollet/Fielding plaque
10. All Saints
11. Crosby Hall
12. Lindsey House
13. Site of Thomas More's house
14. Paultons Square

idea of the type of small town house that once adorned many parts of the metropolis. **Argyll House (3)**, designed by Leoni in 1723, is Number 211 King's Road. A blue plaque on Number 213 commemorates Sir Carol Reed, the film director, and Number 215 was the home at one time of Dr Thomas Arne, who wrote 'Rule Britannia'. In this group can be seen a plaque stating that Ellen Terry, the famous actress, lived here in the 1920s.

We now reach **Glebe Place** and, turning down it, leave the hustle of the King's Road behind us, pausing occasionally to note the different styles of the houses, including many with large studio windows facing north. Just as the street turns sharply to the right note the charming little cottage (**4**) on your left, a gentle reminder that Chelsea was once a little village far out in the wilds of Middlesex. It is reputed to have been a hunting lodge on the estate of Henry VIII. A ceramic plaque on the building relates to the Chelsea Open Air Nursery School that was founded here.

Glebe Place turns and turns again until one finds oneself on the corner of **Upper Cheyne Row (5)**. Here it is worth turning left to admire the houses, again noting that at one of them, Number 22, Leigh Hunt lived between the years 1833 and 1840, while Number 28 displays the date 1767. This whole range is typical of the smaller, cheaper houses built behind the larger ones that once spread along the entire river front by Chelsea Reach.

The Church of Our Most Holy Redeemer and St Thomas More (6) on the corner of Upper Cheyne Row and Cheyne Row, designed by Goldie and opened in 1895, is on the site of the famous De Morgan Pottery Works. It owes its existence to 'an indefatigable missioner and builder of churches – Canon Cornelius Keens'. The building is a complete contrast to the architect's other great church in London, that of St James's, Spanish Place. In Marylebone he chose the Gothic style of architecture, here the Wren-like Italian baroque. The statue of St Thomas More that now stands above the pulpit is by Enzo Plazzotta. It was his model for the competition for a statue outside the old parish church. (The statue of More outside that church is by L. Cubitt Bevis.) Plazzotta generously donated his model to the church.

Architecturally Cheyne Row presents a similar rhythm to that of Queen Anne's Gate near St James's Park Station, dating as it does from c.1708. Like so many streets in Chelsea Cheyne Row claims several famous inhabitants, among them Thomas Carlyle, who lived for nearly fifty years at **Number 24 (7)**. His house, now the property of the National Trust, is regularly open to members of the public from April to October. Among the many treasures shown to visitors is the double-walled room in the attic which kept out the noises of the town while he was working on one of his many books.

26

The statue to Sir Thomas More by L. Cubitt Bevis is inscribed with a replica of More's signature.

It was while living here that he wrote his largest work, *The History of Frederick the Great*, that took him fourteen years to complete. He died here in 1881. There is a bronze statue of him, by Joseph Boehm, in the Chelsea Embankment gardens. It shows him seated wearing his slippers and was erected in 1882.

A short distance from Carlyle's house one comes to **Lawrence Street**, via Lordship Place; although Lawrence House has long since been demolished the street name, from a sub-Lord of the Manor, remains. In this street, like Cheyne Row, many famous persons have lived. Note Duke's House and Monmouth House on the way (**8**), and look hard at the brickwork to find the painted words '6d per night'. Most of the inscription has long since disappeared but it relates to the time when these houses were used as a hostel. Further along, find the blue plaque (**9**) commemorating Tobias Smollet and Henry Fielding, who with John Gay, composer of *The Beggar's Opera*, have helped bring fame and fortune to the street. This is a road of contrasts: compare the Georgian cottages opposite Duke's and Monmouth Houses with the mid-Victorian Peabody Estate buildings on the opposite side of the road.

Return down the street and, facing Duke's House, you will find **Justice Walk**. Halfway along is the old courthouse with the barred gates of the cells underneath. This short walk leads into **Old Church Street**; turn left, and you come to All Saints, the old parish church of Chelsea.

Much of **All Saints (10)** was destroyed during the Second World War and had to be rebuilt. However, thanks to the excellent work of the late Walter Godfrey, only a highly experienced eye will be able to distinguish the restored from the rebuilt. It was in 1528 that Thomas More served as an altar boy here. He also was the parish clerk of the old parish of Chelsea, of which this was the church. The south chapel of the church is one of the earliest works of the Renaissance in the London area. It has a distinctly French atmosphere and is said to be the work of Holbein. Among the monuments in the chapel is one to Thomas More, with the inscription composed by More himself. Tradition has it that his headless body was buried in this chapel. In one corner of the churchyard note the tomb of Sir Hans Sloane, who, besides leaving his name to several streets in Chelsea, gave us the Chelsea Physic Garden and the basic collection of what is now the British Museum, as well as a number of books on botanical subjects. The tomb's urn is made of Coade stone, an artificial stone made in a factory on the South Bank where the Royal Festival Hall now stands. In 1969 a seated statue of Thomas More was unveiled in front of the church. It is the work of L. Cubitt Bevis and shows him, with the chain of the Chancellor on his lap, looking towards the spot from which he took his leave of his family. Inscribed on the front of the statue is a copy of his signature.

Walking in the direction of the bridge seen from the west doorway of the church, one first comes to the **Margaret Roper Gardens**, commemorating More's daughter, who married into the Roper family, and in whose family vault at Canterbury the head of Thomas More was buried.

Danvers Street further on recalls Sir John Danvers, who had a house here and was one of the signatories of the death warrant of Charles I. The gardens at Danvers House were laid out in the early

The Thames and Lots Road Power Station from Battersea Bridge.

part of the seventeenth century, but had disappeared by the end of it.

On the corner of Danvers Street and the Chelsea Embankment, the latter completed in 1871, stands the former hall of Sir John Crosby. **Crosby Hall (11)**, built in 1466, once stood in Bishopsgate in the City, but owing to road-widening schemes and rebuilding at the turn of the nineteenth century it was scheduled for demolition. It was saved, dismantled stone by stone and beam by beam, and brought here. Incidentally, Thomas More lived for a time in Crosby Hall when it was in the City. It is now in private hands and is not open to the public.

Battersea Bridge lies almost opposite the Hall and the present bridge, dating from 1890, replaces the old timber one immortalised in paintings by Turner, Whistler and Greaves. A number of the last artist's works, depicting Chelsea and its associations with the river in earlier days, are in the Museum of London.

Looking upstream from the foot of the bridge one's eyes are arrested by the silhouette of **Lots Road Power Station**, not one of the most glamorous buildings in London, but certainly one of the most useful as it supplies much of the power needed to drive London Transport's complicated network of underground railways. It derives its name from the Common Lots or Lammas Lands where, from August to February, cattle were allowed to graze. Later the area became the famous Cremorne Pleasure Gardens.

Lindsey House was the home of Whistler and the Brunels.

Opposite the foot of the bridge is Cheyne Walk and by turning to the left, away from the side of the church, one finds another interesting group of eighteenth-century houses. Here too is the only remaining large-scale riverside house. **Lindsey House (12),** dating from 1674, is now a tenanted property owned by the National Trust. Permission to visit may be obtained by writing to the tenant at the house. It has one of the finest seventeenth-century interiors in London. It was originally a three-storeyed house but about a hundred years later it was subdivided into its present form. Count Zinzendorf lived here for a time when it became the headquarters of the Moravians in England. Originally founded in Bohemia in the late fourteenth century, the Moravians were a Protestant church. They reached England in 1750 when the Count decided to

30

establish the church in England. He bought land here in Chelsea from Sir Hans Sloane and built a chapel that was attached to their burial ground. The burial ground in **Moravian Close** lies behind the house. In Moravian tradition the area is divided into four squares, one for each category of person, i.e married men, married women, single men and single women. They all had 'their allotted space'. Traditionally they buried their dead both deep and standing upright. No gravestones are visible above the lawn-like ground; there is only a flat stone giving the barest of details of the person buried beneath. Whistler also lived at Lindsey House, as well as Sir Marc Brunel, builder of the Thames Tunnel, and his more famous son Isambard Kingdom Brunel, the engineer of the Great Western Railway.

But we must retrace our steps from the foot of the bridge and turn left up into **Beaufort Street**, walking up the very line of the avenue which led to Beaufort House, where Thomas More lived until that fatal day in 1534 when he was taken by boat to the Tower of London. Today the site **(13)** is occupied by Allen Hall, a Roman Catholic seminary, and all that remains in the area from More's time is an old mulberry tree under which, it is said, he used to sit and meditate.

Continuing to walk up Beaufort Street, one comes, once more, to King's Road. Turn right and pass a number of interesting squares, of which **Paultons Square (14)** rates a special note, being an excellent example of a town square of the 1830s with terraced houses built on a unified plan. In a few minutes you will find yourself back at the former Chelsea Town Hall.

Walk 4
Fleet Street and its tributaries

Temple Bar—Prince Henry's Room—St Dunstan's-in-the-West—Johnson Court—Gough Square—Fleet Street — Cheshire Cheese—Salisbury Square — St Bride's Church—Ludgate Circus.

Until the mid 1980s Fleet Street meant newsprint and memories of great writers like Dr Johnson. Yet the street has more to offer than journalism and gossip. Few people may know of the noble houses belonging to the bishops and abbots which, before the Reformation, once lined the street between the city and Westminster. Even fewer realise that the name springs from a hidden river flowing down from London's northern heights to enter the Thames near Blackfriars Bridge – the river Fleet.

Fleet Street begins and ends at its western frontier at **Temple Bar (1)** where this walk commences. Here are the first, and the last, buildings – if we are to believe street numbering. Once the western gates of the city were at Newgate and Ludgate, but some time before 1293, London stretched itself out to Holborn and Temple Bars. No one knows exactly when; the date is only relevant to the first recorded mention of the expansion. Temple Bar was an office for the collection of tolls and duties and a barrier against rogues entering or leaving. Being on the direct route between the city and the Palace of Westminster, it was also the place where the sovereign paid (and still pays) due respect to the power and might of the citizens of London. Many old prints portray Temple Bar and there is a bas-relief on the present-day plinth that stands in the roadway. Wren built that gateway between 1670 and 1672. Apart from the traditional uses, it served, in its time, as an office for Child's Bank, as the local lock-up, and as a pincushion for a set of gruesome spikes upon which well-known and freshly executed heads were placed. Temple Bar was demolished in 1878, after nearly a hundred years of agitation for its removal, being re-erected sometime later on the estate of Sir Henry Meux at Theobalds Park in Hertfordshire, where it remains to this day. (One possible solution to the problem of the traffic and Temple Bar was to raise it over the roadway by means of an iron structure.) The memorial now standing in its place, causing as much obstruction to traffic as did the Bar, bears on its top a dragon representing the City of London.

Child's Bank is Number 1 Fleet Street, within yards of the

Walk 4. Fleet Street and its tributaries

1. Temple Bar
2. Middle Temple Lane
3. Prince Henry's Room
4. St Dunstan's-in-the-West
5. Johnson's Court
6. Dr Johnson's house
7. Ye Olde Cheshire Cheese
8. Pepys plaque
9. St Bride's
10. Edgar Wallace plaque

plinth, most unbanklike in appearance but with a long history. Founded by Sir Francis Child, the first goldsmith to become a banker, its customers have included Charles II, Nell Gwynne and Samuel Pepys, whose accounts can now be examined in Glynn Mills Bank in Lombard Street. Charles Dickens transformed Child's into Tellson's in his *A Tale of Two Cities*. The bank still retains a memory of its earlier days, before street numbering became the rule, for we can see outside 'the sign of the Marigold'.

Moving on now, a little to the right is a large classical frontage serving as the entrance to the **Middle Temple (2)**. This gateway, often attributed to Wren, was designed by Roger North, an amateur architect and a bencher, and bears on the keystone a lamb and flag, emblem of the Middle Temple, and '1684', the year of its construction. There is a little balcony and below are great studded doors. A peep through into Middle Temple Lane, which divides the Inner from the Middle Temple, reveals a scene straight out of the 1690s with a row of houses complete with overhanging upper floors.

Returning to Fleet Street, opposite Chancery Lane one sees another relic of old London, **Prince Henry's Room (3)**, with its Jacobean gabling and double overhang, a building of 1610 which may have been used as the office of the Duchy of Cornwall under

33

Prince Henry, son of James I – hence the title. Serving once as a waxworks exhibition and later as a public house, today it is maintained by the City of London Corporation. Entrance is free but restricted to between 11 a.m. and 2 p.m., Monday to Friday, and the room, with a magnificent ceiling and panelled walls, is well worth a visit. There is also an exhibition arranged by the Samuel Pepys Club of London. The archway below leads into the Inner Temple.

A few more steps and on the left-hand side of the roadway we arrive at **St Dunstan's-in-the-West (4)**, so called to prevent confusion with a church dedicated to the same saint on the other side of the City. Looking at the top of St Dunstan's for the first time one is struck by the tower's singularly beautiful architecture. St Dunstan's was built in 1829-33 by John Shaw to replace another which had to go as a result of Fleet Street being widened. (It is hardly the widest of thoroughfares even now.) First mentioned in a document of 1185, the church is closely associated with two great preachers: William Tyndale, who first translated the New Testament into English and who was martyred, in 1536, and John

*Middle
Temple Lane.*

34

Prince Henry's Room overlooks Fleet Street.

Donne, the famous dean of old St Paul's Cathedral. Izaak Walton, a parishioner and biographer of Donne, had his classic *The Compleat Angler* published from the churchyard and there is a window to his memory in the present octagonal church. Some of the statuary embellishing the 1586 Ludgate at the time of its demolition in 1760 was removed to St Dunstan's, like the fine statue of Queen Elizabeth I now seen over the vestry porch. Perhaps the passer-by is more impressed with the bracket clock, one of London's best-known. Made in 1671, every hour it causes the two club-bearing figures to strike the bell. This clock was removed to a villa in Regent's Park and returned to Fleet Street only in 1936. Today the church is also used by various Orthodox congregations.

Staying just long enough to witness the free entertainment from the clock, look now over the road to Number 37. This is **Hoare's Bank**, another very old-established private banking company. Like Child's it also retains its street sign, in this case a golden leather bottle, though some say it is really a leather wallet representing the lowly origins of the bank's founder, who, so the story goes, came to London with all his worldly possessions stowed away in such a purse. An old tradition here is that a member of the

Hoare's Bank with its leather bottle sign in the balcony over the door.

Hoare family always spent one night a week sleeping on the premises.

The bank's left-hand edge carries a blue plaque indicating that the **Mitre Tavern** was once Hoare's next-door neighbour. This was one of the favourite haunts of Dr Johnson, who in this pub once dandled some attractive Methodist maidens on his knees in an effort to win them away from their new-found faith! The Mitre was old in Johnson's time for Samuel Pepys went there twice in 1660. In 1788, four years after Johnson's death, the Mitre closed its doors.

We come next to **Fetter Lane**, possibly named after the beggars or fewters who once frequented it, or perhaps after the feltmakers or *feutriers*. On the other side of Fleet Street there is Mitre Court. This court too is an entrance to the Temple. Then comes another opening, this time marked 'Sergeant's Inn', a memory of the time when the highest order of barristers, the sergeants-at-law, held court here until their society was dissolved in 1877.

Meanwhile, on the left (north) side of Fleet Street a series of alleyways awaits exploration and, on finding **Johnson's Court (5),** named after Thomas Johnson, a Merchant Taylor and antiquarian, who owned it and lived here in the fifteenth century, we follow the signs that take us to Gough Square and the delightful late seventeenth-century house (**6**) where Dr Johnson lived for ten years, many of them in great poverty. In the attic the great *Dictionary*, his literary triumph, was written and in this house too his wife died. The great conversationalist and wit, first Parliamentary journalist, poet and novelist who became Fleet Street's most famous personality, left this house in 1759. The house is open to visitors from Monday to Saturday on payment of an entrance fee. Later, Johnson moved into Johnson's Court, where he lived from 1765 to 1776, during which time he met James Boswell. Ultimately he was given the greatest posthumous honour his country could offer, burial in Westminster Abbey.

Leave Gough Square by any of the alleys leading back to Fleet Street and then cross to the south side. Turn into Bouverie Street and find – with difficulty – **Magpie Alley**. Walk through and at the end turn left into Whitefriars Street; within a moment **Britten's Court** will be seen on the left. We stop here because below, in the basement of the office building, is the only surviving piece of the Whitefriars monastery, in which lived the Carmelite Friars from 1241 to 1538. Strangely, the Act of Dissolution ordered by Henry VIII causing the monastic buildings to be demolished overlooked the right of sanctuary, and the area rapidly became the home of every sort of criminal. Known to Londoners as Alsatia, this unsavoury district, though destroyed in the Great Fire, was not to have the anomalous privilege of sanctuary removed for another thirty years.

Re-enter Fleet Street at the top of Whitefriars Street and almost opposite is the little entrance to the alley called Wine Office Court. Over its entrance you will see a lamp indicating that you have discovered Fleet Street's most eagerly sought-after pub, **Ye Olde Cheshire Cheese (7)**. It was rebuilt in 1667 after the Great Fire, so many of the fixtures and fittings are of that date. Most taverns were built or rebuilt at this time because the city could not rise again unless its builders were provided with refreshment! The Cheshire

Cheese claims a Dr Johnson's chair, though it is unlikely he ever sat on it here, and in the cellar a bricked-up doorway hides an alleged tunnel under Fleet Street which, before the days of Henry VIII, allowed miscreants to seek sanctuary in the nearby Whitefriars monastery.

Return to Fleet Street again and at **Number 147** is a statue that would make our earlier acquaintance, Queen Elizabeth I, turn in her grave: it is of Mary, Queen of Scots, who, at Elizabeth's command, spent nineteen years in prison before being executed in 1587. The building here is called after her family name, Stuart House.

Continue down the hill to Peterborough Court on the site of the palace of the bishops of Peterborough. Opposite is **Salisbury Court**, which we enter, keeping a look-out for the blue plaque **(8)** on the side of the Reuter building which marks the birthplace of Samuel Pepys, civil servant and London's best-known diarist. The little street opens into Salisbury Square, once the centre of the huge complex lived in by the bishops of Salisbury.

This same side has a passageway leading directly into Fleet Street's most beautiful building – the church of **St Bride's (9)**. Believed to have given the western world its spire as a model for all wedding cakes, Wren's St Bride's is the pride and joy of Fleet Street. Arisen from the ashes of its pre-blitz predecessor, Wren would not fault any of the modern ideas incorporated in the renovations and would have been amazed at what the archaeologists found below. For here are the remains of all the earlier churches on the site as well as a portion of a Roman pavement and any visit to St Bride's should take in the crypt, which has been turned into a museum of living history *in situ*. In this church Pepys was baptised, and Samuel Richardson, author of *Pamela*, was buried, as was the man who first brought printing to Fleet Street over 400 years ago, Caxton's pupil, Wynkyn de Worde.

The history of the United States is linked with St Bride's too; apart from the spire's lightning conductor being the centre of a dispute between Benjamin Franklin and George III, there are also close associations with those who sailed away to become the founding fathers of the New England states. In the corner of the church, near to the font, there is a terracotta bust of a young girl. This work of Margery Meggitt commemorates the first child to be born of British parentage in North America. Her maternal grandfather was John White, who sailed to America with Sir Walter Raleigh in 1585. White was an artist and samples of his work can be seen in the Bloody Tower at the Tower of London.

St Bride's was the 'parish church of the Press' and received the benevolence of all those who worked in the street and this is reflected in the magnificent interior. For the passer-by, however, it is the exterior, with the loftiest spire in the City, which dominates the scene.

Walk on now, past the graveyard with its burials piled high above ground level; note on the left the rear of Ye Olde Bell, another tavern of 1667, and turn left into Fleet Street again. Opposite is **Poppins Court**, where once stood the London house of the abbots of Cirencester, whose sign was the poppinjay.

At last we arrive at Ludgate Circus and the valley of the now sewered-up river Fleet. Turn left and you will immediately see the memorial plaque to **Edgar Wallace (10)**, the Fleet Street journalist who wrote thrillers. Almost opposite was once the site of the notorious Fleet Prison, described in Dickens's *Pickwick Papers* and shown so vividly in Hogarth's *Rake's Progress*. Not least amongst its more famous prisoners was William Penn, Quaker and founder of Pennsylvania. Part of the London scene since the days of the Normans, destroyed during the Great Fire and again during the Gordon Riots of 1780, the Fleet Prison was not completely demolished until the 1840s. But no matter how buildings come and go, Fleet Street and its tributaries will always attract the visitor.

The wedding cake spire of St Bride's church.

39

Walk 5
The Precincts of Westminster Abbey

St James's Park Underground Station—Queen Anne's Gate—Dartmouth Street—Tothill Street—Broad Sanctuary—St Margaret's Church—Old Palace Yard—Millbank—Dean Stanley Street—Smith Square—Lord North Street—Cowley Street—Barton Street—Great College Street—Dean's Yard—Westminster Abbey.

To most people's minds mention of Westminster Abbey will either bring back memories of coronations that have taken place there or remind them of the tombs and monuments of the famous within its walls. But the area around the Abbey is equally interesting; there are many intriguing places nearby normally missed by those who are overwhelmed by the Abbey itself.

Westminster Abbey has been on its present site for 900 years; indeed, if tradition is to be believed, a heathen temple here was converted to Christianity in the second or third century AD. It stands on a one-time island in the estuary of one of London's lost rivers, the Tyburn, which rises in Hampstead and empties into the Thames near this spot. It was originally called Thorney Island because this was the nature of the place. Not, one would have thought, the best of neighbourhoods in which to build an abbey or, for that matter, a royal palace. The story is told that one evening two fishermen casting their nets in the Thames thereabouts were beckoned to by a figure on the southern shore. They went over to him, and he asked them for a passage across to Thorney Island. On the journey he revealed that he too was a fisherman and that he had come to dedicate the church that was to bear his name. This, it was claimed, was St Peter coming back to earth for the occasion! It is said that the Abbey was never consecrated by a mortal because of this event! Certainly the monks of Westminster put great store in the story by claiming a tithe (a tax) on all the fish caught in the river by Thorney Island. Today the Abbey has much to offer students of history and architecture, showing as it does all the styles of the Gothic periods. However, we are not here concerned with the Abbey but with the area surrounding it, through which we intend to walk.

The starting point for our walk is **St James's Park Underground Station (1)**, in itself an interesting building. It houses the headquarters of London Regional Transport and used to have one of the most famous telephone numbers in the London Telephone

Walk 5. The precincts of Westminster Abbey

1. St James's Park station
2. Queen Anne's Gate
3. Queen Anne's statue
4. Palmerston plaque
5. United Nations plaque
6. Broad Sanctuary
7. Middlesex Guildhall
8. St Margaret's church
9. Roman boundary stone
10. Houses of Parliament
11. Jewel Tower
12. Henry Moore sculpture
13. St John the Evangelist
14. Lord North Street
15. T. E. Lawrence plaque
16. London House of St Edward
17. Dean's Yard
18. Abbey Bookshop

Eighteenth-century houses in Queen Anne's Gate.

Directory: ABBey 1234, now 0171-222-1234. It offers a twenty-four hour service from which you can get almost any information regarding transport in the London area: 'How long will it take me to get to...?', 'What is the time of the last train tonight from . . .?', 'Will you please send me a set of your maps which will make my stay in London more profitable?' The building, to the design of Charles Holden, was erected in 1929 and the famous sculptors Jacob Epstein and Eric Gill were commissioned to do the figures on the outside. Before commencing the walk take a look at the building and see the various sculptures on it. Cross the roadway, stand outside the Old Star public house and look up. Here can be seen the east, south and west wind sculptures. Around the corner on the other side of the wing the east, north and west winds blow.

At the lower level opposite the public house is Jacob Epstein's 'Night', with his 'Day' around the corner.

At the side of the station's main entrance is the street called **Petty France**. This may have originated from the settlement of French refugees who came here after the signing of the Edict of Nantes in 1685, but there is the suggestion that the name is older by a century or more because of French wool merchants who lived here in the sixteenth century. Cross the road and walk towards Queen Anne's Gate, pausing, after having crossed the road, to look back at the Holden building and noting how wide, by comparison, the roadway is at this junction. The street is called Broadway because, with the construction of nearby Victoria Street in 1845, many small alleys and slums were swept away to make this splendid wide road.

Shortly **Queen Anne's Gate (2)** turns sharply to the right and one is immediately back in eighteenth-century London. This is a street which shows the elegance of that age in its houses. Originally the first section had a brick wall at the far end and was known as Queen Square; beyond, where the road narrows slightly, was Park Street. Today they are one street. Take particular note of the keystones of the arches over the windows. They are made of Coade stone, an artificial substance manufactured by the Coade family at their factory which stood where the Royal Festival Hall now is on South Bank, near today's Waterloo Station. The formula of the compound was lost with the death of the last member of the family in the early nineteenth century. But the beauty of the work remains, and when one realises that many noted sculptors were involved in carving the moulds in which these stones were cast it is clear that the manufacturers strove for perfection. It is ironic too that modern scientists are unable to analyse the compound since Coade stone is one of the few substances impervious to London's atmosphere. Note also the ornate overmantels of the doorways; these are often painted to look like stone or plasterwork.

Where the road narrows you will find **a statue of Queen Anne (3)**. Originally it was to have graced a column at the west end of the church of St Mary Le Strand, which James Gibbs was then building. The Queen's death, however, on 1st August 1714, put an end to the idea. Instead, the church was given a steeple and Queen Anne's Gate got the statue.

Notice across the road a blue plaque **(4)** indicating the birthplace of Lord Palmerston, Prime Minister of Great Britain.

At the end of Queen Anne's Gate turn right into Dartmouth Street and passing the Fabian Society headquarters on the right you will come to **Tothill Street**. A 'toothill' is a place suitable for a stronghold, and we read in the Authorised Version of the Bible, in the Second Book of Samuel, how David 'took the totehill of Zion', which Wycliffe translates as the 'stronghold of Zion'. Tothill Fields has a long and sometimes macabre story to tell, the site being used for ordeals by battle, executions and burials. In the parochial accounts for the parish of St John the Evangelist, Westminster, there is mention of '67 loads of soil for the graves of Tothill Fields wherein 1,200 Scotch prisoners taken in fight at the Battle of Worcester were buried'. In the fourteenth century the Gatehouse Prison was built on the Fields and here Sir Walter Raleigh spent the last night before his execution in 1618 in Old Palace Yard, Westminster. In 1690 Samuel Pepys, the famous diarist, was detained in the Gatehouse, having been accused, falsely as it was later proved, of being 'affected to the King'. It was finally demolished in 1776, but not before having the wrath of Dr Johnson brought upon it for the foul condition in which the prisoners were kept.

At the end of Tothill Street one sees across the road Westminster Abbey, in whose immediate precincts we have now arrived. Before crossing the road into the area of Sanctuary we should note the plaque (5) on the wall of the **Methodist Central Hall**, which informs us that this was the venue for the early sessions of the United Nations Organisation. Built in the early part of the twentieth century in French Renaissance style, for the sum of £250,000, it has the third largest dome in London. In addition to the great central hall, which has seating for over 2,000 people, there are offices and banks built into the side of the building. The late Sir Robert Perks, Liberal Member of Parliament and devout Methodist, was largely responsible for its construction. The site was previously occupied by the Aquarium, for many years a London pleasure haunt. Opposite is the Queen Elizabeth II Conference Hall, opened in 1986.

Crossing the road, but keeping on the opposite side of the road from Westminster Abbey, we enter **Broad Sanctuary (6)**. The first record of a sanctuary here was in the last quarter of the twelfth century. Briefly, a sanctuary was a place to which criminals could escape and live in safety, providing their crimes were not treasonable or anti-church. They had to agree to keep the rules of the sanctuary but apart from this were at liberty to come and go as they pleased. A now demolished street outside Sanctuary was called Thevenlane or Thieves Lane.

Cross the road towards the church which stands in the shadow of Westminster Abbey; look back for a moment and you will see the former **Middlesex Guildhall (7)**, reminding us that Westminster was once the County City of the County of Middlesex. Just along on your right you will find the entrance to the churchyard of **St**

St Margaret's, the parish church of Westminster, is used by members of Parliament.

Margaret's (8), parish church of Westminster. The original church was built at the time of Edward the Confessor, *c*.1064, to accommodate the people of Westminster who had been sharing a part of the abbey church with the monks, but with whom they were always quarrelling. The present building is of the early sixteenth century, and is an excellent example of a late Gothic church. Since 1614 St Margaret's has been the parish church of the House of Commons and in 1735 Parliament assumed responsibility for some repairs that needed doing at that time. The windows commemorate people of a wide variety of talents. The west window, given by citizens of the United States of America, shows scenes from the life of Raleigh, who is buried near the High Altar; there are also memorial windows to Saxton the cartographer, Milton the poet, Blake the Puritan admiral, who is buried in the churchyard (his grave is unmarked), and many others. But perhaps the most curious and interesting of all is the east window of Flemish glass. It was a gift to Henry VII from Ferdinand and Isabella of Spain, whose daughter Catherine of Aragon married Henry's eldest son, Prince Arthur. Later, when Arthur died, Catherine became the wife of Arthur's brother, Henry VIII. Prince Arthur and Catherine are shown in the bottom half of the window, but neither saw their portraits here. After passing through a number of hands Parliament purchased the window in 1758 and installed it in its own church. By the side of the west tower is the modern porch and opposite in the grass of the churchyard you will discover a **Roman boundary stone (9)** embedded in the ground. It has the Roman numeral IIL on it and marked the extent of the jurisdiction of the governor of Roman London.

Taking the pathway with St Margaret's on your left and the Abbey on your right, you will come to **St Margaret's Street;** turn right and, passing the eastern chapels of the Abbey on your right,

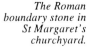

The Roman boundary stone in St Margaret's churchyard.

The Victoria Tower of the Houses of Parliament.

you will come to the statue of George V opposite Old Palace Yard. Look across the Yard at the vast expanse of what was formerly the Royal Palace of St Stephen at Westminster, now more popularly called the **Houses of Parliament (10)**.

Opposite the tall Victoria Tower you will find, on your right set back from the road, the **Jewel Tower (11)**. Thought by some to have been the Abbot of Westminster's prison, its uses over the past 700 years have been various. It certainly must have formed part of the old palace, destroyed by fire in 1834, because in the fourteenth century it was used as a depository for the private jewels and treasure of Edward III. Much later it became a store-house for the records of the House of Lords, and in the nineteenth century the Tower was used by the Weights and Measures Department. The

In Lord North Street there are still signs to public air-raid shelters, relics of the Second World War.

roof was destroyed in the Second World War, but since then the whole building has been restored and fish once more swim in the clear waters of its moat. The Jewel Tower is open to visitors throughout the year.

We walk on, passing on the left the Victoria Tower Gardens with the statue of Mrs Pankhurst, great champion of Votes for Women, and further back a replica of Rodin's famous sculpture 'The Burghers of Calais'. We shall also see, on our right, a fine abstract by Henry Moore (**12**), entitled 'Knife-Edge Two-Piece' (1965).

Soon we reach Dean Stanley Street, and there turn right, shortly to find ourselves in **Smith Square**, dominated by Thomas Archer's former church of **St John the Evangelist, Westminster (13)**, now used as a concert hall. It was built in 1728 as one of the Fifty New Churches of Queen Anne's reign. Dickens, in *Our Mutual Friend*, describes the church 'generally resembling some petrified monster, frightful and gigantic on its back with its legs in the air'. There is the story that when asked what sort of church she would like the architect to build, Queen Anne kicked over a stool and said 'Build me one like that!'. Actually the four corner towers support the rest of the building between them and, bearing in mind that this land is very marshy, it is not surprising that Archer had to use such methods to stop the church from sinking into what had once been the river bank.

Turning to the right when entering the square one can walk round two sides of the church, and at the same time admire the lovely remaining eighteenth-century houses.

One of the ways out of the square is by the charming eighteenth-century **Lord North Street (14)**. Note the 'Public Air Raid Shelter' signs on some of the houses in the street.

Lord North Street crosses Great Peter Street, leads into Cowley Street and then into Barton Street. Note, towards the end of this last, on the left-hand side, the blue plaque commemorating Lawrence of Arabia **(15)**, who lived in this house until his untimely death in a motor-cycle accident.

This trio of streets leads us to Great College Street, and looking to the right, one sees the outside wall of the old monastic precinct of Westminster Abbey. Turn left and you will be passing alongside one of the many monastic houses in London today, the red brick **London House of St Edward (16)**, of the Society of St John the Evangelist. This is the oldest order for men of the Church of England, having been founded in the latter part of the nineteenth century; thus within the shadow of the old Abbey of Westminster thrives a new monastery! Immediately opposite is a pair of iron gates leading into **Dean's Yard (17)**, part of the jurisdiction of the Abbey. Dean's Yard contains, amongst other places, Church House, the parliament house of the Church of England, and Westminster School, a famous London public school. The boys play cricket or football, according to season, on the centre grass plot, which is out of bounds to visitors. In the far corner of the Yard there is a gatehouse. Pass through this and you will find yourself at the west end of Westminster Abbey. Ahead is a tall granite column, designed by George Gilbert Scott, on the top of which stands the figure of St George killing the dragon. The inscription around the foot reads 'To the memory of those educated at Westminster School who died in the Russian and Indian Wars AD 1854-1859'. To your right is the **Abbey Bookshop (18)**, which, after having walked around the Abbey's precincts, is well worth a visit.

Walk 6
In the steps of the Black Friars

Blackfriars Underground Station—Mermaid Theatre—St Benet's Church—Queen Victoria Street—Godliman Street—Knightrider Street—Carter Lane—Dean's Court—Wardrobe Place—St Andrew's Hill—Ireland Yard —Playhouse Yard—Church Entry—Carter Lane—Blackfriars Lane—The Black Friar public house.

In the early part of the thirteenth century a group of black-robed friars attached to the Order of St Dominic settled in London on land now occupied by Lincoln's Inn. By 1276 they had become a prosperous community and moved to a larger site at Thames-side adjacent to Baynard's Castle. There they built a church, cloisters and other priory buildings; later they even had their own quay. Highly favoured by Edward I, who buried the heart of his Queen Eleanor within the precincts (the rest of her body was put in Westminster Abbey), Blackfriars was used for other royal and noble interments. On three occasions Parliament met within its walls, one of them, in 1523, being the session when Sir Thomas More was made Speaker. More was also present at the so-called Black Parliament of 1529 which took place at the priory when, for the first time, he clashed with Henry VIII over the King's proposals for a divorce from Catherine of Aragon. Within four years black friars were being executed over the same issue and in 1538 the end came with the priory's surrender. From that time until its destruction during the Great Fire of 1666, the priory buildings and lands were in the possession of the nobility and their sub-tenants, some of whom we shall become acquainted with on the walk.

Outside **Blackfriars Station** turn left to the widest road bridge (1) across the Thames, opened in 1869 by Queen Victoria, whose statue is nearby. Although London has had other bridges built since then none has been as wide as Blackfriars – a rather sad commentary on progress!

Return to **Blackfriars Station (Thameslink) (2)** and walk upstairs to the booking hall. This rebuilt terminus and offices overlook the river and the Castle Baynard development. At the entrance to the platforms can be seen stonework from the former station's doorways. They are inscribed with the names of places which were served from Blackfriars. From here you could book to Berlin or Sevenoaks or other destinations.

Continue past the station and cross the roadway by way of the

Walk 6. In the steps of the Black Friars

1. Blackfriars Bridge
2. Blackfriars Station
3. Mermaid Theatre
4. St Benet's church
5. College of Arms
6. Horn Tavern
7. Shakespeare plaque
8. Former St Paul's Deanery
9. Wardrobe Place
10. St Andrew-by-the-Wardrobe
11. Priory remains
12. St Ann's graveyard
13. Priory plaque
14. Society of Apothecaries
15. Thameslink incline
16. Black Friar tavern

Blackfriars Bridge is the widest road bridge across the Thames.

subway to the **Mermaid Theatre (3)**, a venture started in 1959 by actor-producer Bernard Miles. The Mermaid was the first permanent theatre to be built in the City of London since the sixteenth century. Its plays are performed in what was an old warehouse-cum-prison serving the adjacent Puddle Dock. The theatre is now enclosed within a modern office building.

Between the theatre and the river is Upper Thames Street. Both this and its eastern partner, Lower Thames Street, follow the line of the Roman riverside defensive wall. Almost every excavation along this Roman thoroughfare has yielded enormous amounts of archaeological material, indicating that the Romans had built many villas by the Thames.

After the Norman Conquest this section of the riverside was occupied by the gaunt and forbidding Baynard's Castle. Not so well-known as the Tower, it was one of three strong fortifications (the others were the Tower and Montfichet Castle) built to defend and protect Norman London. Originally built by one Ralph Baynard, a henchman of William the Conqueror, this castle lasted only until 1212 when it was deliberately demolished by King John after its rebellious owner had fled for his life. On returning to favour, the ex-miscreant rebuilt the place. In 1278 the castle was sold to the Black Friars, but early in the 1400s it was burnt down. Baynard's Castle was rebuilt again, this time a little further east, and in it Edward IV was proclaimed King of England. It continued to play

52

an active role until the Great Fire of London, when it was partially destroyed. The site was not fully cleared until the 1880s. Previous to the recent Upper Thames Street demolitions a blue plaque commemorated the castle, as indeed a local public house still does.

Return to Queen Victoria Street and continue to walk forward to the pretty brick church of **St Benet's (4)** (1677-85), decorated with festoons and topped with hipped roofs. One feels that Christopher Wren put a great deal of affection into its design. The previous church was where Inigo Jones, the seventeenth-century architect, was buried and one ponders over the reason why Wren saw fit not to perpetuate the memory of his great predecessor. Since 1879 St Benet's has been used by the London Welsh Episcopalians. Opposite is Faraday House, the International Telephone Exchange. When it was erected in 1932 there was a public outcry, with letters to the national newspapers condemning the height of the building so near to the cathedral. It was, and is, nine storeys high!

Cross the main road to the **College of Arms (5)**, fronted by a magnificent pair of gates picked out in black and gold, presented to the College in 1956 by an American benefactor. The College is a tight corporation consisting of three Kings of Arms (Garter, Clarenceux and Norroy & Ulster), who are assisted by six Heralds (York, Richmond, Windsor, Somerset, Lancaster and Chester) and four Pursuivants bearing the romantic titles of Portcullis, Rouge Dragon, Rouge Croix and Bluemantle. They work under the direction of the Earl Marshal of England, traditionally, since 1672, the Duke of Norfolk, even though he is not a member of the College. They arrange state ceremonials, design coats of arms, check pedigrees and family trees and work in all those fields where heraldry still holds court. Their attractive building in mellow red brick dates from 1671, being one of the tiny handful of non-religious post-Great Fire buildings to survive. The site was originally occupied by Derby House, which was acquired by the College of Arms in 1553.

Leave the College on your right, turn right into Godliman Street and again right into **Knightrider Street**. This is a very old name, first heard of in a document of 1332, perhaps derived from the route taken by the knights who, fully armed for the tournament, would come along here from the Tower on their way to the jousting grounds at Smithfield. However, our reason for entering Knightrider Street is to see the **Horn Tavern (6)**, rebuilt to the original design and well-known to Charles Dickens. In *The Pickwick Papers*, he made it the meeting place of Messrs Snodgrass, Tupman and Winkle, who came here to purchase a bottle or two of good wine which they afterwards took to the nearby Newgate Prison, where Mr Pickwick was temporarily incarcerated.

St Benet's church, designed by Sir Christopher Wren, in Queen Victoria Street.

Walk back to Godliman Street, turn right and then left into **Carter Lane**. After a few yards you will find a wall (at right angles to the pavement) upon which is a plaque (**7**) reminding us that William Shakespeare was resident in this district. This is merely the first indication of Shakespeare's presence in the precincts of Blackfriars.

Carter Lane is very narrow, with numerous sub-streets and alleys leading off. One feels that this sector was left untouched by the Great Fire and this is how London used to be. But Wren's grandiose schemes were ignored and much of London was rebuilt without any alteration to the street plan. Only the houses were different, built more of brick than timber. Now, much of this district is to disappear in a new wave of town planning, and walking amidst the many empty buildings around here one is perhaps taking a last look at old London.

A few yards past the Shakespeare plaque turn right into **Dean's Court**. Here, on the left, behind two gates stands the former Deanery of St Paul's Cathedral (**8**), a delightful well-proportioned 1670 Wren house, its doorcase framed with garlands – a very picturesque scene spoilt only by the general gloominess of the immediate surroundings.

Back down Carter Lane again, turn right. On our right is a long building, once the St Paul's Choir School, in a style that Sir Nikolaus Pevsner jokingly calls 'South Kensington'. The external walls were embellished with religious motifs and floral decoration not unlike the sort of thing one sees in northern Italy – ideal for a sunny clime but not for the smoke-begrimed London of the mid 1870s. The building is now used by the Youth Hostel Association (YHA).

Look now for Number 57 Carter Lane a little further on (it is opposite the former Choir School) and there you will find an entrance into **Wardrobe Place (9)**. This humble-looking oasis, endeavouring, as it were, to escape its environs, has a history worthy of its attempts to survive. For here in medieval times was the King's Wardrobe, established by Edward III, where were kept the ceremonial robes of state, on view to the public just as the Crown Jewels are today. Therefore it was, in a way, a museum though it seemed to have another and more mysterious role, because in 1604 William Shakespeare received $4\frac{1}{2}$ yards of scarlet cloth from the Wardrobe enabling him to attend the state entry into London of James I. Samuel Pepys, too, was a visitor to the Wardrobe on more than one occasion though he must have been among the last because in 1666 the building was destroyed in the Great Fire, and not rebuilt. In 1709 the office of the Wardrobe was abolished and the garden of the great house was converted into this pleasant little courtyard.

Into Carter Lane again, turn left, and left into St Andrew's Hill, past the elegant eighteenth-century rectory on the left, to the church of **St Andrew-by-the-Wardrobe (10)**, a few yards further on. This is another Wren church, of 1692. In its early days it was called St Andrew's-by-the-Castle, referring to Baynard's Castle. Like so many of Wren's buildings in red brick it is very attractive and our view of it, so close to the rear, is by no means the best. It is a high church, both spiritually and physically, the latter because of the 1869-71 cutting of Queen Victoria Street which left the building perched so high above pavement level. St Andrew's was gutted by incendiary bombs during the Second World War but it has since been beautifully restored.

Return to St Andrew's Hill. Opposite is **Ireland Yard**, which we enter. We are now in the depths of what was once the Blackfriars Priory complex. This alley is named after William Ireland, one of the sub-tenants of the previously dissolved priory buildings. On the right there is a small clearing in which can be seen the only remaining piece of the great priory left above ground (**11**). An inscription on the garden's outside wall tells us this was once part of the priory's dorter or dormitory.

Ireland Yard opens into **Playhouse Yard**; this is all that remains of the famed Blackfriars Theatre. Opening in 1577 as London's second official playhouse, it has often been confused with the better-known and slightly later Blackfriars Theatre of James Burbage. The latter building occupied the so-called Parliament Chamber of the priory and from its start met with opposition from its aristocratic neighbours. Later, James's son Richard took over both the building and the players, as part of a syndicate which included John Hemming, Henry Condell and William Shakespeare. Certainly the last had most of his plays performed here. The Blackfriars Theatre became the winter home of the group; in the summer they played at the Globe on the other side of the river. By 1642 the Puritans had gained control of the area and the Blackfriars was ordered to close down; in 1655 the theatre was demolished.

Just before entering Playhouse Yard we would have seen a little alley called Church Entry. A few yards up there is the little graveyard of **St Ann's, Blackfriars** (**12**) (another fragment of the same churchyard was the clearing off Ireland's Yard). St Ann's was originally the parish church of the precincts of the priory. During the period when the theatre was next door a constant stream of complaints was made to the Burbages about the theatre's trumpets, drums and acclamations drowning the services. The church perished in the Great Fire and was never rebuilt. Oddly enough, in 1905, the famous architect Banister Fletcher was commissioned to build a new St Ann's Vestry Hall in Edwardian Baroque style a yard or two away. In the Vestry Hall are the offices of the Ancient Monuments Society, founded in 1924 'for the study and Conservation of Ancient Monuments, Historic Buildings, and Fine Old Craftsmanship'.

Go now to the top of Church Entry, left into Carter Lane and left into Blackfriars Lane, passing a blue plaque (**13**) to Blackfriars Priory on your left. Some little way down, on your left, is the entrance to the hall of the City livery company **the Society of Apothecaries** (**14**), in a building of 1670 and 1786 containing a very beautiful main hall in panelled black oak. This was one of the very few company halls to survive the Blitz. The Apothecaries

In Ireland Yard is the last visible piece of Blackfriars Priory.

used to be classed with the Grocers because of their background of herbs and suchlike remedies, but as time passed a real division occurred and in 1617 they received a Royal Charter of their own. Since the nineteenth century the Society has been an examining body in medicine and surgery and, in consequence, a Licentiate of the Society is qualified to be a general practitioner. Its coat of arms, seen over the doorway, is surmounted by a rhinoceros and is supported by two unicorns, the horns of both beasts being highly prized once for their medicinal properties.

We make our way down Blackfriars Lane, where on the right-hand side can be seen the incline of the railway line leading up to Blackfriars Station (**15**). The line is the Thameslink enabling passengers to travel from Bedford, through London, to the south coast without having to change trains.

At the end, turn right into Queen Victoria Street, and just past the railway bridge on the right is London's most highly decorated pub, **The Black Friar** (**16**). Covered from top to bottom in Art Nouveau by H. Fuller Clark and Henry Poole, the theme, inside and out, is of conviviality and jolly friars. There is even one fat friar pointing the way to the saloon bar – which perhaps is not such a bad idea!

Walk 7
Mayfair – on the course of the Tyburn

Green Park Underground Station—Piccadilly—Whitehorse Street—Shepherd Market—Curzon Street—Queen Street, Mayfair—Charles Street—Berkeley Square—Hill Street— Farm Street—South Audley Street—Grosvenor Square.

During the first two weeks of May for many years an annual fair was held in a suburban London field which was to stamp its name on the richest square mile in all Britain outside the City of London. From its earliest days, even before it was transferred from the Haymarket, the fair was notorious for wantonness and in its later years was to be called 'a nursery of Vice and Atheism'. The great development of the West End during the mid eighteenth century brought about its eventual closure, for the wealthy and influential citizens who came to live within earshot were able to nullify even a fair held under the rights of a royal charter. Thus Mayfair began to change to its present form, though many of the fair's features survived and on the walk a sharp eye will soon detect them!

Starting from **Green Park Underground Station**, we walk along Piccadilly towards Hyde Park Corner keeping the park on our left. The name of this roadway has somewhat cloudy origins; but the Middlesex county records of 1623 tell us that there was a large house near today's Piccadilly Circus belonging to a Mr George Baker, a tailor. He sold at his shop a fashionable accessory called a pickadil, a sort of ruff sometimes worn on the collar or about the hem of a garment. Soon his house became known as Piccadilly Hall.

It was only one of the many large mansions that lined the road to Hyde Park. Indeed, the Green Park Station is on the site of a great house which once belonged to the Duke of Devonshire. The second street along is Clarges Street. Turn in a yard or two and on the right at Number 1 is the **Kennel Club**, the repository of every canine pedigree in the United Kingdom and elsewhere.

Back into Piccadilly, turn right, and on the Park side of the road we can see a magnificent pair of wrought-iron gates, picked out in blue and gold. In the early eighteenth century they fronted Lord Heathfield's house at Turnham Green, but in 1837 they were purchased by the Duke of Devonshire to gate his exquisite Chiswick House. He later fixed them to the frontage of his Piccadilly mansion and in 1921, just prior to demolition, the gates became part of Green Park's railings.

Walk 7. Mayfair – on the course of the Tyburn

1. Naval and Military Club
2. Whitehorse Street
3. Shepherd Market
4. Dartmouth House
5. Running Footman
6. Clive of India's house
7. Church of the Immaculate Conception
8. Goodes
9. Grosvenor Chapel
10. Purdey's
11. Grosvenor Square
12. US Embassy

Crossing Half Moon Street, a few yards further on is one of the great Piccadilly landmarks, popularly known, because of the giant lettering on the gateposts, as the IN and OUT Club, but in reality the **Naval and Military Club (1)**. It was founded in 1862 by five officers who decided, rightly, that there was room in London's Clubland for another services club. Within three years they had outgrown their premises and bought Egremont House. It has been their home ever since that time. Today the house is also home for a number of other clubs including the former Bath Club, as well as the Ladies' Carlton and the (Ladies') Cowdray Club. With the closure of The Goat membership was increased by some thousand naval officers. This typical example of a West End town house dates from 1756-60 and was once lived in by the Duke of Cambridge and, later, by Queen Victoria's Prime Minister Lord Palmerston. We see only the frontage. Continuing down the slope of Piccadilly, Whitehorse Street is reached.

One immediately notices that **Whitehorse Street (2)** is out of character with the rest of Piccadilly's side streets. Narrow and winding, it follows the course of a now disappeared tributary of the Thames, the river Tyburn. Though very small, this river played a large part in London's history, its estuary forming the two arms between which Westminster Abbey was sited. It rises in Hampstead on the northern rim of the London Basin, forms a lake in Regent's Park, crosses Oxford Street (at which point in medieval days it was tapped to provide the City of London with some of its water supply), shapes not a few of Mayfair's streets including Whitehorse Street, forms the valley of the western end of Piccadilly, flows under Green Park and below Buckingham Palace and on to the Thames at Westminster.

Whitehorse Street opens out into **Shepherd Market (3)**, the very heart of Mayfair and the site of the earlier charter fair. Consisting of the minute square we are now in, an even tinier piazza and a few surrounding streets, it is Piccadilly's quaintest backwater. Owned, designed and laid out in 1735-46 by Edward Shepherd, it is a reminder of how carefully the eighteenth-century speculators considered their tenants: shops, a market, a chapel (now gone) and taverns. A petite self-contained village it was and still remains. Not so long ago it was one of the most notorious 'red-light' districts in London, until an Act of Parliament swept 'the girls' off the street. Despite the changes Shepherd Market is still one of the great off-beat sights of London, picturesque and lively, with pretty little restaurants and a fascinating street life, if we are to indude the many tourists who flock here just to take photographs. And if you have time to spare, have a drink in Shepherd's and perhaps a meal in Tiddy Dol's.

At Number 6 Queen Street, Mayfair, Prince George lived with the showgirl he married.

Now go through one of the two archways and enter **Curzon Street**. Opposite will be seen a most irreverent-looking Third Church of Christ, Scientist, as well as two adjoining and interesting little shops. The first is Trumper's, the gentlemen's hairdresser, unique in its austere, not over-modern, window display and the three coats of arms, indicating that royal haircuts have been provided. The other is Heywood Hill, the bookseller, considered the home of the literary establishment, where many notables obtain their current reading.

Turn left, cross Curzon Street and enter **Queen Street, Mayfair**. (This is the proper name of the street: to omit the affix would create confusion!) Number 6, on the right, was once the home of Mrs Fitzgeorge, a lady of some importance who greatly disturbed Queen Victoria. As Louisa Fairbrother, a 'light entertainer', she was secretly to marry Prince George, heir to the Duke of Cambridge. The Queen was furious but was unable to invoke the Royal Marriage Act, as her discovery was three sons too late! So the sons were disallowed title inheritances; reference books failed to mention Mrs Fitzgeorge, as she was called and since the ducal home was barred, they lived in Queen Street, Mayfair. She died in 1890 after fifty years of happy marriage. Only in 1935 did the royal family ever visit Number 6, when Queen Mary came to sort out the heirlooms of this morganatic marriage.

At the top of Queen Street, Mayfair, turn right into **Charles Street**, which epitomises the whole area – enormous eighteenth-century houses with plain, even dirty, black exteriors, but sumptuously decorated interiors. Distinctly aristocratic, they are still lived in by people of immense wealth who prefer a town house in the West End rather than a large house in Hampstead, Kensington or Belgravia.

Number 37, on the right, is **Dartmouth House (4)**, the London headquarters of the English-Speaking Union. It is also the home of the Royal Society of St George, whose aims include fostering the love of England and strengthening England and the Commonwealth by spreading the knowledge of English history, traditions and ideals. Originally three houses, it was converted in 1890 by Lord Revelstoke into one very large mansion. Note the attractive architectural trimmings and some fine ironwork. The English-Speaking Union has been here since 1918 and exists to draw together and give assistance to all those who speak the English language.

Further along on the left, on the corner of Hays Mews, we come to a pub whose name is unique. **'I am the only Running Footman'** (5) says the sign, and that is the official title. It was the job of this personal servant to run ahead of a nobleman's coach, to pay tolls, assist passengers to alight and at night to carry the flare. He could run at 7 miles (11 km) an hour and would refresh himself from the top of his wand which carried wine and egg-whites. Such menials were common enough in the seventeenth century but this pub commemorates the last of them. The fourth Lord Queensbury, who gave this place its name and who died in 1810, was the last nobleman to exploit his servants in this wretched manner.

Continue along Charles Street and at the end, where we turn left, we are in lovely **Berkeley Square**. The massive plane trees, some

The plane trees in Berkeley Square are over two hundred years old.

of the largest in London, were planted in 1789 and somewhere in their branches sings the fabled nightingale. The square is called after the Berkeley family, who owned much of this part of the West End in the seventeenth century. There was a time when it was purely residential and as such exceeded Grosvenor Square for sheer wealth. Now the residents have all gone and only a few of the old noble houses remain. Walking up the gentle slope of the Tyburn valley, and noting the fine ironwork outside some of the older houses, we come to **Numbers 45-46 (6)**, a pair of good stone-faced buildings believed to have been designed by William Chambers, an architect of the Georgian golden age. Clive of India lived here, as the blue plaque denotes, as did Henry Flitcroft, another great Georgian. William Kent was responsible for **Number 44**, considered to be the finest terrace house in London, and though the exterior now looks as new as the day it was built it gives the passer-by no idea of the splendour within. Inside there is the grandest of grand staircases, not to mention many beautiful rooms. Kent built this house in 1742-44 for Lady Isabella Finch, though today it has become the Clermont Club, sometimes known as Aspinall's, where, should you wish, you can lose a fortune in style. In short, it is the most aristocratic gambling club in all England. Even the basement has a glory of its own, for here is Annabel's, a night-spot for the famous.

Turn left into Hill Street, and then right into **Farm Street**, following it round to the left. Farm Street is basically a mews, where once the nobility kept their horses, carriages and coachmen in cottages. The twentieth century, however, has seen these properties converted at enormous cost into the most dazzling of small town houses. The result is that Farm Street is now well worth lingering in.

We have now entered the estate of the Grosvenors. This family came into possession of this area in 1677 when Sir Thomas Grosvenor, Baronet of Eaton Boat, at twenty-one years of age married Mary Davies, aged twelve years and eight months, heiress to the fabulously wealthy Audleys. The marriage laid the foundation of the largest and richest estate in Westminster. As long ago as 1880 their descendants were drawing £1,000 a day in ground rent, though their Mayfair lands were but a small portion of their total holdings.

Farm Street has, on the right, two buildings of interest. The first bears over its doorway a large coloured coat of arms of the City of Westminster and serves as one of that council's street cleansing depots! The second, the grey-stone **Church of the Immaculate Conception (7),** is of more than usual interest. Here is no ordinary Catholic place of worship, for this is the London church of the Jesuit Fathers, an order of great importance within the Catholic body politic. Built in 1844-9 by J. J. Scholes, with a high altar by the famous Victorian architect Pugin, the church has a superb interior, numerous chapels of great beauty and an east window in stained glass by Evie Hone (1953).

Continue into South Street and turn right at South Audley Street. At this corner is **Goodes (8),** a china and glassware shop that claims to be the largest in the world. Certainly it is one of the more impressive Mayfair businesses and is typical of many in this area in that it is run by a dynasty. Founded in 1827 by a former tax-collector, William Goode, the shop is now controlled by his descendant. The main entrance has a very clever mechanical device which throws the doors open when the step is trodden on, pre-dating our modern electronic-eye gadgets by a half century or so. It is often referred to as the 'Elephant Shop' because of the two richly decorated china elephants to be seen in the windows. They were made by Minton for Messrs Goode and shown at the Paris Exhibition of 1889. The family has resisted all offers to sell them.

On the next block will be seen (best viewed from across the road) the simple and homely **Grosvenor Chapel (9).** Originally a so-called proprietory chapel, this was built by Benjamin Timbrell in 1730 as part of the great Grosvenor Square scheme. Such chapels were built as a speculation based on pew-rents; they were not usually consecrated and Holy Communion could only be celebrated by licence from the local bishop. This one seems thor-

Grosvenor Chapel was built in 'Colonial' style in 1730.

oughly out of place, looking as if it should be in New England. Indeed, the style is called Colonial, and one feels that when the American servicemen worshipped here during the Second World War they must have felt very homesick. Earlier regulars included the elderly Florence Nightingale, who lived around the corner in South Street. The vaults, sealed for a hundred years and their exact whereabouts a mystery, contain the remains of John Wilkes, who fought for the liberty of Englishmen, and of Lady Mary Wortley Montague, writer, wit and friend of Pope, Addison and other notable literary and society figures.

Opposite at Number 57 is a local curiosity, **Purdey's**, the gunmakers (**10**). This is another dynastic business, brought here from Oxford Street in 1826 by James Purdey, being persuaded to

Purdey's are the pre-eminent makers of sporting guns.

do so by the first Duke of Westminster, one of the Grosvenors. James built this place as a picture-gallery just in case the gun business failed. However, guns were a great success, but the Long Room, as it is called, is a gallery filled with portraits of four generations of aristocratic customers and appears to be a delightful compromise.

Finally, we enter **Grosvenor Square (11)**, which with its 6 acres (2.5 hectares) is London's largest. It was laid out in 1695 by Richard Grosvenor, occupying the site of Oliver's Mount, an earthwork thrown up for the defence of London when Charles I was advancing after his Edgehill victory (hence, nearby Mount Street). By 1725 the square had been filled with very large houses and extremely wealthy tenants.

Grosvenor Square has long been associated with North America, and one of the first residents during the years 1731-43 was Charles Calvert, fifth Lord Baltimore and the hereditary proprietor of Maryland. But the first citizen of the USA to live in the square was John Adams, later President of the United States, though when he and his daughter Abigail lived at Number 9 (which house is still standing) he was then only America's first minister to Britain. From then on the square became a favourite place for visiting

Americans, the peak being reached during the Second World War when it was tagged 'Eisenhowerplatz'. Because of these associations the square was chosen as the site for W. Reid Dick's statue of Franklin Delano Roosevelt and the fine likeness was unveiled by Mrs Roosevelt in 1948 in the presence of George VI.

During the late 1950s the whole west side was demolished to make room for Eero Saarinen's massive **United States Embassy (12)**, a very good piece of modern diplomatic architecture with a 35 foot (10.7 metre) long eagle spreading itself on the roof's edge.

In the north-west corner of the square stands the statue of Dwight David Eisenhower (1890-1969) by Robert Dean. The gates on the south side, Diplomatic Gates, commemorate the Treaty of Paris, 1783. Just by the gates is a memorial to the Eagle Squadron of the Second World War, 1939-45.

Walk 8
The Great Fire of London

The Monument—Monument Street—St Mary at Hill—Eastcheap—Philpot Lane—Lime Street—Leadenhall Market—Leadenhall Street—Cornhill—St Peter's Church—St Michael's Church—St Michael's Alley— Castle Court—Ball Court—Birchin Lane—Change Alley—Lombard Street—King William Street—The Monument.

On the night of 1st September 1666, Thomas Faryner, one of the king's bakers, went to bed little realising that he was to play an important part in the history of the City of London. He was awakened, some two hours later, by thick clouds of smoke pouring into his bedroom from the bakery downstairs. His daughter and maidservant sleeping in other rooms nearby were also disturbed in their sleep. The bakery was on fire ... Faryner saw that their way of escape down the stairway was impossible, so he took them to the upper rooms of the house and they made their escape through an attic window. The little maidservant was too terrified to jump on to the roof of the next house, and so became the fire's first victim.

It had been a dry summer and soon, with the help of a fierce wind to the east, neighbouring houses caught fire; shortly after, the whole street was ablaze. The fact that a nearby inn had a stack of dry hay in its courtyard did not help matters.

Meanwhile, the fire had attracted the attention of some city officials including the Lord Mayor, Sir Thomas Bludworth, who was reported as saying 'a woman might piss it out'. In fairness to the Lord Mayor, fires were no new thing for the city; the past history of the city was full of them, but, as he was later to realise, this was to be no ordinary fire.

Another noted citizen wakened by the fire was Samuel Pepys, whose diary entries for this period contained some of the finest descriptions, but he too regarded it as just another fire and went back to bed.

Next morning, however, the situation had worsened, and people were beginning to take a serious view of the fire. In fact, it was to rage for three days and three nights before it was contained, and even then there were further small outbreaks over the period of the next week or so. One later diarist recorded, a year later, that smouldering timbers were still being found buried under the rubble of what had once been the very fine and noble City of London.

The Great Fire made thousands of people homeless, burned five-sixths of the city, and caused many to think again about the so-

Walk 8. The Great Fire of London

1. The Monument
2. Pudding Lane
3. Walrus and Carpenter
4. Watermen's Hall
5. St Mary at Hill
6. St Margaret Pattens
7. Mice carving
8. Leadenhall Market
9. Standard of Cornhill plaque
10. St Peter-upon-Cornhill
11. St Michael's, Cornhill
12. George and Vulture
13. Simpson's Chop House
14. Birchin Lane
15. Garraway's plaque
16. St Mary Woolnoth
17. St Clement, Eastcheap

The plaque in Pudding Lane which recalls the origin of the Great Fire of London.

called fire precautions of London. It also gave a golden opportunity to 'that miracle of youth, Doctor Christopher Wren', as Evelyn described him, to formulate plans for a new City of London. Even before the flames of the fires had abated Wren was presenting his plans for the city's rebuilding to King Charles II. So did several other 'amateur architects', but to no avail; their plans did not even reach the city fathers for consideration. But what did emerge from this great fire was a series of beautiful, rebuilt churches and a magnificent St Paul's Cathedral, all in the new Renaissance style of architecture.

To walk from one extreme of the fire to the other would take too long, but to explore the area that the fire consumed in the first twenty-four hours is far more practicable.

Let us begin this walk at the **Monument (1)**, just a few yards away from the Monument Underground Station, in itself a constant reminder of the Great Fire of 1666. It stands 202 feet (66 metres) high, which is the distance from its base to the site of the house in Pudding Lane where the fire started, and is the work, basically, of Sir Christopher Wren. Built between 1671 and 1677 it is a fluted Doric column of Portland stone, and the view from the top is still one of the finest in London. It is necessary to climb 311 stairs to reach the balcony. Nowadays this is enclosed and has been since, amongst others, two bakers and a baker's daughter committed suicide by throwing themselves from the top – an ironic twist of history! Explore around the base of the column and you will find a bas-relief, by Caius Gabriel Cibber, representing London, her destruction and how she will rise again from the ashes of the Great Fire.

Returning to the entrance of the column, let us leave the Monument behind us and walk down Monument Street, pausing when we reach **Pudding Lane (2)** to note this insignificant byway which played such an important part in the City's history. On the corner of Monument Street and Pudding Lane stands Faryners House. In 1986 the Worshipful Company of Bakers unveiled a plaque on the wall here. The inscription reads: 'Near this site stood the shop belonging to Thomas Faryner the King's Baker in which the Great Fire of September 1666 began. Presented by the Worshipful Company of Bakers to mark the 500th anniversary of their Charter granted by King Henry VII in 1486.'

Continuing, we come to the **Walrus and the Carpenter (3)**, where previously stood one of the public houses serving the former Billingsgate fish market. Next door once stood a café where the fish-porters could get a warm dish of soup, taken from a copper that was never allowed to run dry, always being replenished before it could do so. The soup was delicious! One day the sign 'Under new management' was posted in the windows, and very soon the copper of soup was allowed to run dry. There, in the bottom of the vessel, was an old fish-porter's hat which was promptly removed. The soup never tasted the same...Alas, such hats are no longer seen in Billingsgate today. Made of wood and lined with leather, they protected the porters when they were carrying the heavy boxes of fish on their heads. They were almost exactly the same hats as were worn by archers in the field of battle.

We have now reached **Lower Thames Street** and the junction with St Mary at Hill. Just a few yards up the latter one finds the **Hall of the Company of Watermen and Lightermen of the City of London (4)**. Founded in the sixteenth century to protect all those whose livelihood directly depended upon the river, this well-preserved hall dates from 1786 and is in the style of Adam and Wyatt. On its coat of arms can be seen the crossed oars and the long row-boat used by the watermen and two sacks representing the goods which they would unload from the ships at anchor in the Thames.

Walking up **St Mary at Hill**, one soon comes to the church **(5)** which gives its name to the street. Although not destroyed in the Great Fire it was rebuilt in the latter half of the eighteenth century. John Stow, in his *Survey of the Cities of London and Westminster*, says that St Thomas Becket, London's own saint, was rector here for a time in the twelfth century. Another, though much later, rector was Prebendary Wilson Carlile, founder of the Church Army. In May 1988 a fire destroyed much of the roof and damaged the interior. Restoration is now complete. Before proceeding up the hill note the clock above, controlled by rods from a mechanism to be found in the west tower of the church at the other end of the building.

At the top of the hill, across the road (the junction of Eastcheap and Great Tower Street), stands the church of **St Margaret Pattens** (**6**). Founded originally in 1067, it was severely damaged in the Great Fire and rebuilt by Wren between 1684 and 1689, the steeple being added in 1703. Its curious affix is said to have originated either in the name of an early benefactor, Patins, or from pattens, a type of clog worn over the ordinary shoe in wet weather, which were made in Rood Lane near to the church. The church has pews at the west end bearing the initials 'CW' said to stand for Christopher Wren, until one remembers that they can also stand for church warden!

Outside the church, turn right and walk down **Eastcheap**, but not before noting the very fine Georgian shop fronts on your left just by the church wall. Shortly, on your right, is Philpot Lane. Just

The clock of St Mary at Hill and the steeple of St Margaret Pattens.

*The entrance to
Leadenhall Market.*

a few yards in on your right, look up and find the two grey mice (**7**).
The story is told how one day, when the building was being erected
in the nineteenth century, a workman brought his customary bread
and cheese for his midday meal, laying it down on the scaffold
where he had been working. Suddenly one of his workmates drew
his attention to the food, which was being devoured by two grey
mice. He must have been a kind-hearted fellow for, so the story
goes, he left the creatures to finish his lunch for him and then asked
one of the plasterers to immortalise the story.

Leaving the mice to their cheese, we walk up Philpot Lane, cross
Fenchurch Street, getting its name from the Foin Church, near an
ancient hay-market, and so come to **Lime Street**, which at the
close of the eighteenth century was inhabited by many wealthy city
merchants. Today there is little or nothing to detain us, and so we
walk on to **Leadenhall Market** (**8**), one of London's chief poultry
markets. It stands on the site of the old Leaden Hall, manor house
of the Nevill family, which was later purchased for the City of
London by Mayor Richard (Dick) Whittington. The market dates
from the middle ages, although the present building was erected in
1881 to the designs of Sir Horace Jones, who, a few years earlier,
had also built Smithfield Market. The forum stood here in Roman
times and underneath many of the shops are traces of foundations
of the great basilica (the courts of law and the market and meeting
place of Roman London). Leadenhall Market suffered in the Great
Fire but was not wholly destroyed, thanks to a rich merchant who
threw money to the crowd so that buildings surrounding it were
pulled down to make a break in the way of the flames.

Following through the market and Whittington Avenue on the
other side, one comes to **Leadenhall Street**. Turn left, and in a few
yards you will come to an important junction in the city's roadways.

Here meet Leadenhall Street, Gracechurch Street and Bishopsgate, the exact spot where roads met in Roman times and where, once, London Stone is said to have been. Look up, across Gracechurch Street and you will see a blue plaque (9) indicating that the Standard of Cornhill once stood here.

Cross the road and walk down Cornhill and you will find, on your left, the former parish church of **St Peter-upon-Cornhill (10)**, once claimed to have been founded by King Lucius in 179 AD. In 1979 they celebrated eighteen hundred years of Christianity on this site! Destroyed in the Great Fire, St Peter's was rebuilt by Wren in 1680; its rood screen, one of only two post-Reformation screens, is said to have been the personal work of Wren, because it was in the senior church of the city. The building is now a Christian study centre.

Back in Cornhill once more, and turning to our left outside the church of St Peter, another church is soon discovered: **St Michael's, Cornhill (11)**. This church had a Saxon foundation and in 1055 was given to the abbots of Evesham, who continued to draw tithes from it until the Reformation in the sixteenth century. The present church is by Wren but was much altered in the nineteenth century by Sir George Gilbert Scott. In the churchyard here were buried John Stow's father and grandfather, although there is no longer any trace of their graves. Thomas Gray, the poet, was baptised here, and there are several memorials to the Cowper family who worshipped at St Michael's.

We have now reached one of the city's most intriguing 'backdoubles', St Michael's Alley, leading us to more interesting places behind the busy streets. But first we track down, on our left in St Michael's Alley, a blue plaque informing us that here was London's first coffee house, the Pasqua Rosee (the Easter Rose). A junction is now reached; on the right is the **George and Vulture Tavern (12)**. Before the Great Fire there were two taverns, one the George, which claimed to be the oldest in the city, having been converted in the twelfth century from an ordinary house into an alehouse, the other called the Lively Vulture. After the fire they were amalgamated. Stories regarding its long and interesting history are innumerable but the one told most often refers to Charles Dickens, discovering the George and Vulture on one of his walking tours of the city and throwing his hat up in the air, overjoyed that he had found another quaint old tavern to put in his books. Thus it was that Mr Pickwick and Sam Weller stayed at the George and Vulture for some little while before departing for Dingley Dell.

Retracing our steps a few yards, we turn down Castle Court, finding on our right Ball Court, which, although it is a dark entry

A wooden pelican of 1775 in St Michael's, Cornhill.

The George and Vulture tavern features in Dickens's 'The Pickwick Papers'.

appearing to lead nowhere, takes us down to **Simpson's Chop House (13)**, a perfect 1757 eating house, almost untouched and unspoiled since the day it was first built.

Returning to Castle Court once more, we turn right and, passing under an archway, find ourselves in **Birchin Lane (14)**. The lane first appears in the records of 1286 and takes its name from a local landowner. This is one of a number of thoroughfares coming under the restriction of the City of London Metropolitan Street Act of 1867. This Act forbids you to drive a vehicle of more than four horses down such a street, nor may you carry down it, by hand, any object longer than 36 feet (10.9 metres) or wider than 8 feet 6 inches (2.6 metres). We, however, unloaded and on foot, need not worry but must look for Change Alley across the road.

Change Alley was previously called Exchange Alley because two of its five openings led into Cornhill and the Royal Exchange. We enter by Birchin Lane and soon find, on our right, another entrance bearing a blue plaque on its corner stating that the Marine Society was founded here. Opposite is yet another plaque, this time in stone, pinpointing the site of the famous **Garraway's Coffee House (15)**, one of the first city merchants to sell tea, at prices ranging from 16 shillings to 50 shillings per pound. Incidentally, next door to Garraway's was Jonathan's Coffee House, the original rendezvous of the stockbrokers and jobbers who were later to form the City of London Stock Exchange. Either exit on your left will bring you to **Lombard Street**, the 'street of the greatest credit

The plaque to Garraway's Coffee House.

76

St Mary Woolnoth, designed by Nicholas Hawksmoor.

in Europe', as a writer once put it, reminding us that here the bankers of Lombardy held forth daily for the purpose of lending money. Hanging signs project from the walls of several of the buildings. One sign shows a grasshopper with the initials TG and the year 1563, being the date of the foundation, by Thomas Gresham, of a bank here. Another shows a cat playing a fiddle and hangs at the site of the Cat and Fiddle inn. One accepted interpretation of the name recalls a knight, Caton, who was highly praised for his valour while fighting at Calais. He became known as Caton le Fidèle, and this was one of the many inns called after him.

77

Turn right down Lombard Street, and at its junction with **King William Street** you will find the church of **St Mary Woolnoth (16)**. The first documented evidence for this church dates from the end of the twelfth century, but the foundation may well be Saxon, in which case it might have received its affix from a Saxon or Danish benefactor; alternatively, there may have been a medieval benefactor with such a name. It survived the Great Fire but in 1717 was demolished and rebuilt by Nicholas Hawksmoor, one of Wren's pupils; there is a distinct influence of Vanbrugh, in whose offices Hawksmoor also worked for a time. Edward Lloyd, owner of the seventeenth-century coffee-house that was to launch Lloyd's of London, was buried in the old church. When the Bank Underground Station was built below the church in 1901 there were storms of protests, but today no one seems to notice.

King William Street was constructed between 1831 and 1835, forming part of the road system from the city to south London, via London Bridge. It was considered by some to be one of London's greatest improvements but today most of the buildings in the street date from the turn of the nineteenth century. At the far end one finds little Clement's Lane with its Wren church of **St Clement, Eastcheap (17)**, replacing a structure of the thirteenth century destroyed by the Fire. This church is one of the two churches contending to be the St Clement's referred to in the famous nursery rhyme.

Ignore the complex road junction, cross King William Street and the end of Cannon Street, then turn right with King William Street in the direction of London Bridge. Walk through the subway to Lower Thames Street and back to the Monument, where, not so long before, we began our search for the first day of the Great Fire of London of 1666.

Index of places

Abbey Bookshop 49
Aldersgate 8
Aldwych 18
Allen Hall 31
All Saints, Chelsea 28
Anne, Queen, statue 43
Argyll House 26
Ball Court 74
Barber Surgeons' Hall
    10
Barton Street 49
Battersea Bridge 29
Baynard's Castle 52
Beaufort Street 31
Bell Yard 23
Berkeley Square 62
Birchin Lane 76
Bishopsgate 74
Black Friar inn 57
Black friars 52
Blackfriars Bridge 50
Blackfriars Lane 57
Blackfriars Station 50
Blackfriars Theatre 56
Britten's Court 37
Broad Sanctuary 44
Broadway 43
'Burghers of Calais' 48
Bush House 18
Carey Street 23
Carlyle's House 26
Carter Lane 54
Central Hall 44
Change Alley 76
Charles Street 62
Cheapside 13
Chelsea Town Hall 24
Cheyne Row 26
Child's Bank 32
Church House 49
City of London police
    station 12
Clare Market 19
Clement's Lane 78
Clive of India's house 63
College of Arms 53
Cornhill 74
Cripplegate 11
Crosby Hall 29

Curzon Street 61
Danvers Street 28
Dartmouth House 62
Dean's Court 55
Dean's Yard 49
Duke's House 27
Eagle Squadron
    memorial 67
Eastcheap 72
Eisenhower statue 67
Elsing Priory 11
English Speaking Union
    62
Faraday House 53
Farm Street 63
Fenchurch Street 73
Fielding and Smollet
    plaque 28
Fetter Lane 37
Fleet Prison 39
Fleet Street 32
Fore Street 11
Garraway's Coffee
    House 76
Gatehouse Prison 44
Geo. Fred. Watts
    Memorial Cloisters 8
George and Vulture 74
George V statue 47
Glebe Place 26
Goodes 64
Gough Square 37
Gracechurch Street 74
Great College Street 49
Green Park 58
Gresham Street 9
Grosvenor Chapel 64
Grosvenor Square 66
Hoare's Bank 35
Horn Tavern 53
Houses of Parliament 47
Immaculate Conception,
    Church of 64
Ireland Yard 56
Jewel Tower 47
Johnson, Dr Samuel
    (house) 37, (statue)
    16
Johnson's Court 37

Justice Walk 28
Kennel Club 58
King's Road 24
King William Street 78
Knightrider Street 53
Law Courts 14
Lawrence of Arabia's
    house 49
Lawrence Street 27
Leadenhall Market 73
Lime Street 73
Lincoln's Inn 22
Lincoln's Inn Fields 20
Lindsey House 30
Lombard Street 76
London House of St
    Edward 49
London School of
    Economics 18
London Wall 9
Lord North Street 49
Lots Road Power Station
    29
Lower Thames Street 11
Magpie Alley 37
Marconi plaque 5
Margaret Roper Gardens
    28
Mary, Queen of Scots
    statue 38
Mayfair 58
Mermaid Theatre 52
Middlesex Guildhall 44
Middle Temple 33
Mitre Court (Fleet St) 37
Mitre Court (Wood St)
    12
Mitre Tavern 36
Monmouth House 27
Monument 70
Moravian Close 31
More, Sir Thomas,
    statues 23, 26
Museum of London 9
Naval and Military Club
    60
Newcastle House 20
New Hall 23
Noble Street 9

INDEX OF PLACES

Old Chelsea burial ground 24
Old Church Street 28
Old Curiosity Shop 19
Old Hall 22
Our Most Holy Redeemer and St Thomas More, Church of 20
Palmerston's birthplace 43
Pankhurst, Mrs, statue 48
Parish boundary stones 23
Pasqua Rosee 74
Paultons Square 31
Pepys, Samuel, birthplace 38
Petty France 43
Philpot Lane 72
Piccadilly 58
Playhouse Yard 56
Poppins Court 39
Postmen's Park 8
Prince Henry's Room 33
Pudding Lane 71
Purdey's 65
Queen Anne's Gate 43
Queen Elizabeth II Conference Hall 44
Queen Street, Mayfair 62
Queen Victoria Street 53
Roman boundary stone 46
Roman city wall 11
Roosevelt, Franklin, statue 67

Royal College of Surgeons 22
Royal Courts of Justice 14
Running Footman 62
St Alban's tower 12
St Andrew-by-the-Wardrobe 55
St Anne and St Agnes 9
St Ann's, Blackfriars 56
St Benet's 53
St Botolph's, Aldersgate 5
St Bride's, Fleet St 38
St Clement Danes 16
St Clement Eastcheap 78
St Dunstan's-in-the-West 34
St Giles, Cripplegate 10
St James's Park station 40
St John the Evangelist, Westminster 48
St Margaret Pattens 72
St Margaret's Street 46
St Margaret's, Westminster 45
St Martin le Grand 45
St Mary at Hill 71
St Mary Woolnoth 78
St Michael's, Cornhill 74
St Paul's Deanery 55
St Peter's, West Chepe 13
St Peter-upon-Cornhill 74
Salisbury Court 38
Salisbury Square 38

Sardinia Street 19
Sergeant's Inn 37
Seven Stars 23
Shepherd Market 60
Ship inn 20
Simpson's Chop House 76
Six Bells 24
Smith Square 48
Soane's Museum 20
Society of Apothecaries 56
South Audley Street 64
Standard of Cornwall plaque 74
Temple Bar 23, 32
Tothill Street 43
Tyburn river 60
United States Embassy 67
Upper Cheyne Row 26
Upper Thames Street 52
Victoria Tower Gardens 48
Wallace, Edgar, plaque 39
Walrus and the Carpenter inn 71
Wardrobe Place 55
Watermen's Hall 71
Westminster Abbey 40
Westminster School 49
Whitehorse Street 60
Wood Street 12
Ye Olde Cheshire Cheese 37
Youth Hostel Association 55